THE INTELLIGENT WOMAN'S (USED) CAR BOOK

Confident Car Ownership Made Easy!

S. Thomsen

The Intelligent Woman's (Used) Car Book
Copyright © 1998 Oregon Wordworks
ISBN: 0-9625960-6-X

By S. Thomsen

Editors: Barbara Adams, Gayle Chavez, Penelope Frey, Carol Kuehn, Osha Reader and one special woman who chose to remain nameless.

Illustrated by Asher Donaldson, courtesy of the Osborne Gallery, Manzanita, Oregon 97130

Printed in the United States of America
All rights reserved. No part of this book may be reproduced in any form without written permission from the publisher, except for brief quotations embodied in critical articles or reviews.

Limits of Liability and Disclaimer
This book has been prepared based on the author's 25 years of experience in and around the car business, personal expertise, and the feedback of countless business associates, customers and friends. The author shall not be liable in any event for incidental or consequential damages in connection with or arising out of the use of information contained in this book.

"He" includes "she" in all cases but the specific.

Table of Contents

Acknowledgments	v
Introduction	1
1. First things First	9
2. Going in Prepared	45
3. Private-Party Sales	83
4. Miles per Gallon vs. Miles per Dollar	93
5. Special-Interest Cars	102
6. The Trade-In	131
7. Dealer Auctions	137
8. The "Book" and its Mystery Unraveled	149
9. Warranties	165
11. Insurance	173
12. Financing	189
13. Planned Obsolescence	201
14. Check It Out--The Part That Shows	215
15. Check It Out-- Under the Hood and Under the Car	235
16. The Test Drive	263
17. What to Do When it Breaks	279
18. Keep It Running (Nearly) Forever	323
About the Author	339
Quick-Reference Guide	343
Index	349

Acknowledgments

I want to express my appreciation to the six women without whose patient, careful and thorough editing help, The Intelligent Woman's (Used) Car Book would not be. These particular women were selected because of their diverse uses for, interests in and attitudes about their cars, cars in general, and all the things having to do with cars. All of them said they learned a lot from reading the material and all of the material reads a lot better because of their efforts.

Barbara Adams lives in rural Hawaii. Really rural Hawaii. She is a professional bureaucratic problem-solver, mediator and mentor to those in need. She especially likes to see how many miles she can squeeze out of her cars before Hawaii's notorious rust finally claims them. She says that one of the most useful tools to keep in her car at all times is her sense of humor. Her editing contribution was primarily in the areas of content and concepts and was especially valuable because of her expertise in keeping cars like old Pintos with football-sized rust holes running as long as possible.

Gayle Chavez also lives in Hawaii and has lived here so long that I won't even mention she's a transplant from Southern California. She is thirty-something, has her own business and drives her tiny car a lot. She uses it for business and pleasure, loves it almost as much as her cat, enjoys driving and gives her car impeccable care. She makes sure that it is always serviced on schedule and her precious car is always spotless. I picked her as an editor because of her enthusiasm about her car, because of the way she takes care of it and not incidently, for her excellent command of English. She has a better-than-average grasp of the basics of both a car and of the human mind (BS in Human Services and graduate work in Psychology), so her suggestions on anything that she found difficult to understand were especially valuable.

Penelope Frey is a mid-thirties computer software instructor and makes her home in Huntington Beach, California. She has a love for classic and special-interest cars, drives a '69 Mustang (when she's not riding her Harley) and has a feel for things mechanical. She doesn't like the new cars; she feels they have no style or character any more. She added her own unique insight to the editing procedure and made a lot of valuable corrections and suggestions on how to make the material (especially the technical) as clear as possible.

Carol Kuehn, early fifties, lives in the woods of Northern California. She drives a late-model Jeep 4x4 pickup that she bought new because she wanted to "avoid buying someone else's troubles." (That was before she read this book.) She holds a BA in Psychology from Stanford and is a freelance writer as well as an avid gardener and horticulturalist. She uses her truck for all the associated practical reasons. Carol is a stickler for precise grammar, so we went 'round and 'round a few times with some of the liberties I took in keeping the book in a conversational tone. I believe we reached a happy compromise and she finally put away her red pencil. (I think she wore out several.)

Osha Reader, 53, runs a retreat center in the Northern California Sierra. She has two cars, a vintage Porsche that she's owned for nearly thirty years and a new Acura (which she bought before she knew better!). She asked me to add this to her bio: "Like so many other women, I've assumed it was better to shell out ridiculous amounts of money for a new car than to buy a used one that might break down. Skip's book has completely changed this attitude. Now I'm anticipating the exciting special-interest cars I can choose from in the future at a fraction of what I've been paying for new ones."

Osha has a Ph.D. in nutrition and a degree in naturopathic medicine. She is a published author and helped polish and edit the final draft of the manuscript.

And then there is my dear friend who chose to remain **nameless**. She is 42, a recently-retired computer scientist, who has lived in Kansas City for the last twenty years. She owns a Honda Accord that she bought new and avoids driving whenever possible. I picked her as an editor for two reasons: her unique attitude about cars in general and about driving in particular and the fact that she has proven herself to be an editing nitpicker without equal. Her editing expertise focused mainly on content and how it was presented. She found (and I subsequently rewrote) every word, phrase and paragraph that she felt, from a woman's point of view, was unclear, ambiguous or worse.

Last but not least, Cathleen Freshwater, although she was not involved with the final edition that you are now holding in your hand, contributed a lot to the original draft with her editing expertise and tireless support.

Thank you all,
Skip Thomsen

INTRODUCTION

First, why a women's book? In many areas of life, women are the ones who show the true strength of the human species, but when it comes to dealing with any aspect of car-ownership, that just doesn't seem to be the case. With their cars, many women just seem to give up.

During all my years in the business of selling, servicing and repairing cars, it became clear to me that in auto-related dealings, it wasn't just a coincidence that women got burned more often than men. And I learned that it had a lot less to do with mens' "car-savvy" than with the people (almost exclusively men) in the business intentionally taking advantage of women because they *assumed* that women are easy targets. To a lot of women, anything having to do with cars is a "a guy thing," and so they just naturally let the guys make their decisions for them.

But then, most women actively *seek* advice. They listen when they believe the source is credible. Most men already "know everything" about cars, and for sure about wheelin' and dealin'. That's why this book is addressed to women.

And why all this emphasis on *used* cars? Doesn't everybody know that when you buy a used car, you're just buying somebody else's troubles?

Picture this: You buy a brand new car, and after a year something comes up and you *have to* sell the car. It's now a *used* car. Is it going to be a problem for its new owner?

The day you bought it, it depreciated about 30%. By the time you sell it at one year old, it has depreciated up to a whopping 50%! So the new owner gets your $14,000 car for $7000. Who got the better deal, you or the used-car buyer?

Buying used cars is definitely *not* always taking on somebody else's problems. Sure, some used cars have flaws. So do some *new* cars. Used cars that turn out to be lemons are the exceptions, though, and what *The Intelligent Woman's (Used) Car Book* will teach you is how to select a used car that's as good as a new one.

It's not all that complicated, it's not a "guy thing," and once you know the techniques, they will be indispensable to you in keeping your new (used) car running (nearly) forever.

The focus of *The Intelligent Woman's (Used) Car Book* is getting maximum pleasure and utility from your car with a minimum of expense and stress. Saving money by getting a good deal in the first place, never getting taken advantage of on repairs, insurance or any other dealings with your car and by getting the most from your car when you need to sell it. In short, You'll get the most value from your every hard-earned transportation dollar, and have fun in the process. In today's economy, it's important for most of us to use our incomes wisely. Even though it's widely accepted as a fact of life, it's really *isn't* necessary to spend a fortune on your car and on keeping it going. On that premise, I'm addressing primarily the woman who either *cannot* or *will not* spend a large percentage of her income on her transportation.

Going into every aspect of car ownership, maintenance, repairing and insuring, with your eyes wide open, can change forever the way you deal with these issues. It can save you thousands of dollars and a lot of hassles and heartaches. With that comes a confidence and peace of mind that you've probably not known before in your auto-related transactions. The more savvy you are about your car and about how the whole car-business works, the more effective you will be in *your* car-related business. Just your conspicuous confidence will be enough to avert a lot of dubious dealings before they begin. I'll show you how to do it.

In *The Intelligent Woman's (Used) Car Book,* you'll learn to avoid the manipulations in the sales office which often cause customers to pay thousands of dollars more for their purchases than was originally implied. Sadly, this has become industry practice.

Auto dealers conduct seminars and intensive training workshops to teach these tactics to their sales people. Over the years, these training practices have been fine-tuned by professional psychologists skilled in the intricacies of the buying mind.

Against this kind of training, Ms Jane Doe, who buys one car every few years hasn't had much of a chance. Until now!

I'll show you how a lot of efforts to buy an "economy car" usually wind up being anything but economical. You'll learn the important difference between "miles per gallon" and "miles per dollar." I'll even show you how to *avoid completely* the costliest item of car-ownership for most people: depreciation!

You *can* change the way you buy cars. You *can* avoid falling in love in with some flashy ride you wind up married to for the length of the contract, whether or not it serves your needs. You *can* make intelligent decisions before you enter the marketplace, and you can stay within set parameters to find the car you need--and you can do it for a lot less than you ever thought possible!

You'll also learn how to deal with repairs when they become necessary, and even how to get the best mileage from your insurance dollars.

There's no need ever again to be intimidated by the thought of doing business with car dealers or repair shops, or by the guys who think women don't know anything about their cars. Please rest assured that there *are* honest people in the business and good cars out there. I'll show you how to find them.

I purposely didn't include lists of all the cars of recent years that have proven to be lemons. There are already many other books and periodicals available which offer this information. I'm taking over where they left off: instead of asking you to memorize lists of all the defective cars out there, I'll show you how to easily detect deception and smoke out the lemons on your own.

The Intelligent Woman's (Used) Car Book is presented in such a way that you can pick and choose from the table of contents any topic that's of interest to you now. Wherever you read, there will be references to any other chapter that gives further specific related information, and the index will help you easily locate anything discussed in the book. There is no need to read this book in any particular order, although it would be to your advantage to peruse every word sooner or later.

And now, sit back and enjoy your tour of the car business! You're going to learn how to survive all of its rough spots and even how to enjoy yourself in the process.

(The use of the generic "he" when referring to various dealers (and others) is just that: generic. I could as well used the awkward "s/he," but it's too, well . . . awkward.)

FIRST THINGS FIRST

Even when you first start thinking about replacing your car, the thing that comes to mind is assessing your needs. You probably don't need *me* to tell you what you want when looking for a car, but what often happens is that you have a pretty good idea of what you need and how much you want to pay for it and then after talking with a few dozen sales people, your original intentions are forgotten. There are also a lot of little things that sometimes get overlooked in all the excitement of buying another car. They always seem to become more important later: like, why didn't I think of *that*?!?

There are lots of factors, some not so obvious, involved in even the simplest decisions to buy a car. For example, when I bought a car for my eighty-year-old mother, I tried to talk her into a two-door sedan. I figured since she didn't *need* four doors, why be bothered with them. She pointed out that the doors on two-door cars are heavier and harder to open, especially when the car is parked on a bit of a hill. And besides, she said, those long doors on a two-door would be hard to deal with in her skinny garage. I bought her a four-door.

Things to Consider

If you don't already know what your next auto purchase will be, here are some points to ponder.

First and somewhat obvious, are the needs of you and your family, which will decide the size of the car and the number of seats and doors. Then, do you want a hatchback, sedan or station wagon? How about a mini-van or a convertible?

Wagons, all other things being equal, always cost more than comparable sedans. New ones cost more to begin with and there are fewer wagons manufactured in any given model-year. Supply and demand keep the price of wagons higher.

Wagons and minivans are spacious but have the disadvantage of letting whatever you are carrying lie in plain sight of passersby when you're parked. In plain sight also includes in plain hearing; if what you are carrying rattles, you have to endure the noise. To some, noise is very annoying. Wagons, especially smaller wagons, also transmit more road noise into the passenger compartment than do sedans.

You say you'd like a sports car? There are precious few vehicles in today's market that can honestly be called sports cars. Corvettes qualify, as do Mazda Miatas and the very pricey Italian and British cars of racing parentage.

There are a lot of new and late model "sporty" (read: small and flashy) cars available which get billed by their makers, both foreign and domestic, as "sports cars." (I'm an old sports-car nut, and in my humble opinion, it takes more than a few yards of racing stripes and flashy decals to make a sports car.)

In an attempt to avoid the endless controversy about what is and what is not a sports car, let's just call all of those sporty little domestic and foreign numbers "personal" cars. The genuine older sports cars, Triumphs, Jaguars, MGs, Alfas and the like, can still be found. But if one of those is what you really want, you had better either *be* a mechanic or own one! (Maybe a close friend will do.)

The discussions in this book apply to almost any car on the road, but there are some special considerations for exotic cars. If you are entertaining thoughts about buying, for example, a Jaguar, and you are not already intimate with these creatures, have someone who knows them well go over your prospective purchase with a fine tooth comb. (See Chapter 5, "Special Interest Cars.")

One way to be fairly sure that you will find every flaw is to take it to a Jaguar dealer and pay his fee to inspect the car you're interested in. If he also sells used Jags, it will be to his distinct advantage to find every defect possible so that he can sell you one of his. Cars, not defects.

Insurance Issues

One more thing to remember in considering body styles is that in most states, the flashy, sporty models cost more to insure. Your banker or insurance agent has a copy of the tables which show an insurance code giving comparisons of insurance premium costs.

Some cars are more costly to repair than others. Insurers' studies analyze repair-cost comparisons of specific types of collision damage. Then they base their premiums on those findings.

Insurance premiums are also higher on anything that can be called "high performance." The bigger the engine, the higher the premium. This applies to a high-performance image, even if the car is a dog. For example, a garden-variety Camaro with a V-8 engine will often be a "lower risk" than the same year Camaro with a flashy paint job and a name like "Rally Sport"--even if the Rally Sport has a four-cylinder engine.

They also have statistics which show that people who drive those sexy little sports models crash more. (Chapter 11 covers insurance considerations in detail.)

Insurance companies thrive on statistics. Just how valuable are these magical numbers? Consider this: if you had one foot in an oven and the other packed in ice, you would be "statistically" comfortable. So much for statistics.

Big Car or Small?

How big a car should you get? The popular reason for "thinking small" is the generalization that all small cars get better mileage than all big ones. But *some* full-size cars will go as far on a gallon of gas as *some* small ones. Putting a priority on gas mileage alone is often a big mistake, particularly if you have to pay a lot more money for a gas miser than for a bigger car. Yet this is a common rationalization for buying a new car.

Many years ago, when a new VW cost $1695, it might have been possible to make car payments out of the money saved on gas. But most cars built in the last ten years or so get such good mileage that it would be difficult to justify buying a new $10-20,000 car to "save money on gas."

If you're interested in a realistic approach to this decision, it's easy; the arithmetic is pretty basic.

(See Chapter 4, "Miles per Gallon vs. Miles per Dollar")

A more realistic parameter to use in deciding car size is the number and size of the people who are going to use that car, and their comfort. If you're tall, most of the compacts and probably all of the subcompact are going to cramp your body if not your style.

Interior Options

There are seat and interior options that make big differences in comfort, depending on your size, age and personal preferences. We'll get into those in a while.

Seats themselves vary a great deal from car to car. Even within different models of the same make, there are a variety of seat configurations. It's surprising that in all these years of perfecting the automobile, there has been no consensus on an acceptable seat design.

It's a good idea to spend more time than a limited test drive allows to get the feel of the seats in your prospective new car. On long trips, a driver's seat with adjustable lumbar support and backrest angle can't be beat. The driver's comfort is, of course, more important if you often drive long distances than if you rarely go farther than a short commute. Comfort is also more relevant for those whose backs are less tolerant of strained sitting for long periods.

If most of your driving is on the open road and you have a family to transport, a full-sized cruiser might be your best bet, especially one which is a few years old but still in excellent condition. Full-sized cars generally depreciate faster than smaller ones, so an older full-sized car will have been largely depreciated when you buy it used.

Gas Mileage

The gas-mileage question comes up again when discussing the big car. How many miles per year do you drive? The "average" person drives 15,000 miles a year. Since it isn't difficult to find a full-size car capable of 20 miles per gallon, let's use that figure for a comparison.

Let's try some of that arithmetic: Fifteen-thousand miles at 20 mpg would consume 750 gallons of gas. An "average" compact car might get 30 mpg; but let's use a subcompact that gets 35 mpg for our figuring. Fifteen thousand miles at 35 mpg would use 429 gallons. That's a savings of 321 gallons for the year, or 27 gallons per month. Hardly a car payment, right?

Of course, there are other expenses that can be higher in a bigger car, too; notably collision insurance, tuneup and tires. However, collision insurance for an *older* big car will likely be a lot less than for a *newer* small car. And if your bigger old car is more than about six years old, you might be wisest to buy no collision insurance at all. (More on this in Chapter 11, "Insurance.")

Tuneups usually cost more for a V-8 than for a four-cylinder engine but tend to be needed less frequently on bigger cars, especially any cars more than eight or ten years old. And it is almost always less expensive to tune up a simple, easy-to-work-on older car than it is one of the high-tech, ultra-complex, computer-controlled new ones.

Tires will cost more for a bigger car and there's no way around that. You'll need to do some more arithmetic to decide if the extra comfort is worth the price.

A Happy Compromise

If your figures show that the extra cost of operating the big car is more than you feel is reasonable, there is still a way to have your proverbial cake and eat it, too. Find a nice, big, comfortable cruiser with all the toys . . . a few years *older* than you'd been considering. There were some exceptionally fine cars built in the seventies and eighties, and a lot of them are still far from worn out. (See Chapter 5, "Special Interest Cars.") Even at a premium price, a fifteen-year-old car in superb condition will cost a fraction of the price of a five-year-old car in just about any condition.

A fifteen-year-old car has other distinct advantages. Cars were simpler then; any competent mechanic can still service them. Many late-model cars cannot be properly serviced by anyone lacking the correct, incredibly-expensive, dedicated, often dealer-only electronic diagnostic equipment. Not so with the fifteen-year-old auto.

Most older cars have reputations for super-dependability. If you ever bend a fender, a used one for the older car can be replaced inexpensively; not likely with a newer one. And because it is currently unfashionable to drive a big car, even the exceptional ones can be bought for bargain prices.

The happy compromise, evident by its popularity, is the mid-sized car. For example, tall drivers find lots of legroom in cars like GM's Olds Ciera, Chevy Celebrity, Pontiac J-6000 and Buick Century, from about 1982 and up. These cars, nearly identical mechanically, have earned an enviable reputation. With reasonable care and maintenance, they will run well over 100,000 miles with few problems. They perform well and do it all at about 25 mpg. Some of them, like the Olds Cutlass Ciera, has done so well that it remains basically unchanged today.

The only *visible* compromise between these cars and their full-size counterparts is in room to stretch. But there are other differences that are extremely important to some drivers. One is ride. There is no comparison between the ride and handling of Chevy's Celebrity and their Caprice, or between Ford Motor Company's full-size and mid-size cars.

If you aren't familiar with the difference and you already know that you "don't want a big car," I recommend you never drive one. You just might find the luxury of a full-size car irresistible.

There are other, more subtle, differences. The use of plastics for finish trim is more evident in the mid-sized cars. Bigger cars, especially the top-of-the-line models, are just plain plush in ways the smaller cars can only imitate with plastic. This becomes less evident in the newer mid-size cars, especially the "luxury" imports.

Parking huge-mobiles can be a real chore, especially if you're not tall enough to see all four corners of the car. If most of your driving is in the city, and you have to park in skinny little parking places, you need to reach some kind of compromise between luxurious comfort and maneuverability. But if you like a mid-size (or bigger) car, by all means borrow one and try parking it. With a little practice, you can get just about any car into any legal-size space. It just takes a little more skill (read: practice) with a bigger car. The thing to watch is buying a teensy car just for parking-ease, when you would be more comfortable (and safer) in a bigger one. You do, after all, spend a lot more time cruising than parking!

Buy American!

How about the "Buy American" controversy? The controversy sort of dissolves when we look at the facts. A lot of the parts of your Chevy are, in fact, imported. The nuts and bolts that hold the All-American Buick together are *metric*.

When you buy parts for your American car, read the "Made in . . . " tags on them. Just about every manufacturing country in the world is represented on parts tags for American cars. You'll find Taiwan, Japan, Germany, Israel, Canada, Mexico, and other countries all represented. And you'll also find "Made in USA" tags on the parts for Japanese cars!

To further confuse the issue, The apple-pie Geo Prizm is in fact a Toyota Corolla with the name tags changed; the same applies to the Geo Metro, which is a Suzuki Swift; the Chevy Spectrum is an Isuzu I-Mark; a Ford Explorer is the same rig as a Mazda Navaho. Chrysler markets the Eagle Talon and Plymouth Laser; Mitsubishi makes them both and markets their own version as the Eclipse. OK, how about the sporty cars? The snazzy Dodge Stealth is a clone of the Mitsubishi 3000 GT. The Ford Escort is built by Mazda. How about this: The Mercury Tracer is designed in Japan and built in Mexico! Then Toyota's Camry, Avalon, Corolla and their pickups are built in the good old USA, as is the BMW 3-Series and the Z-3. And that's just a short list.

So what, exactly, is an "American car?" Sorry we didn't reach any conclusions on this, except that in today's marketplace, it really doesn't matter.

Options: are they worthwhile?

There are people who still tell you not to get any of those "pesky power-things," because they'll break and cost you lots of money to fix. Matter of fact, only a month ago, I had this beautiful Buick Regal for sale and a woman came along who wanted the car. She really liked it and said she'd go get her husband and they would take the car home with them. It was just what she had been looking for. Well, they returned right on schedule, and as soon as her husband saw that the car had power windows, he said, "No way! Power windows never work right and they're expensive to fix when they break." They didn't buy the car. The punch line: this car was a '79 with 140,000 miles on it; *it was seventeen years old*, and the power windows worked perfectly, as did everything else on this well-maintained car. (And I was selling it for $900!)

I've had a few air-conditioning systems on older cars that needed service, a (GM) power seat or three that didn't work right and maybe two or three power window switches that needed service or replacement. But I've had a lot more manual window regulators that needed to be replaced from rust and corrosion and just as many manual seat-tracks that needed adjustments or repairs to work properly. Most power accessories in cars that have not been abused are extremely dependable, some of the most dependable parts of the car!

Although there are more, we're going to evaluate the following major options and dispel some old myths at the same time:
- Power steering
- Power brakes
- Automatic transmission
- Tilt wheel
- Cruise control
- Power windows
- Power door locks

Power mirrors
Power seats
Split bench seat
Rear defrost
Exotic stereo systems
Air conditioning

POWER STEERING. On anything bigger than a compact, power steering is hardly an option. Even on a lot of compacts, it is valuable if you do a lot of in-city maneuvering and parking. Power steering units have evolved to be so dependable that problems are practically unheard of.

Years ago, people told stories about power steering robbing the engine of five or more horsepower, thus causing a noticeable drop in fuel mileage. *Not true!* The only time that the power steering pump is doing any work at all is when you are actually turning the wheel. Even then the amount of work it does is directly proportional to the force applied to the steering wheel.

In other words, if you turn the wheel quickly from side to side while your car is parked, the pump is working at its maximum for that movement. If you make a long, sweeping turn on the highway, the pump doesn't do a thing. While you are motoring down a long, straight freeway, the pump is merely along for the ride. So power steering is a valuable, dependable, nearly maintenance-free option whose value doesn't depreciate at resale time. As a matter of fact, any *non-power-steering* cars bigger than subcompact are poor investments just because they are very hard to resell when the time comes.

POWER BRAKES. Since most cars have been equipped with front disc brakes for quite a few years now, and most disc brake setups require the use of brake boosters, power brakes have been standard on most cars for years. On new cars, they're still listed as a "no cost option" in many cases, but you couldn't order the car without power brakes if you wanted to.

AUTOMATIC TRANSMISSION. Most automatics are extremely reliable, often still performing like new after well over a hundred thousand miles. On many new cars, they are expensive options.

Since the majority of cars bigger than compacts sold in the last few years have been equipped with automatics, used cars with standard shifts are difficult to find except in a compact or an import not classed as a luxury model. Even some imported "luxury" models have five-speeds.

All other factors being equal, an automatic transmission adds several hundred dollars to the book value of a car less than four years old. The "book" presumes that most cars have automatics, and deducts for a standard shift rather than adding for the automatic. If you're looking for a standard-shift car and find one you like, don't tell the seller. Stick shifts are harder to sell, making a bargaining point in your favor.

Assuming that the automatic transmission will last the life of the car, you could justify the initial extra expense by never needing to replace a worn-out clutch. The average clutch can be expected to last about 70,000 miles. If most of your driving is in the San Francisco hills, figure 40,000 or less, depending on your driving skill.

Of course, if you only commute on freeways fifty miles each way every day, you may *never* wear out a clutch. But if you do, you can count on spending from three to five hundred dollars to renew a worn-out clutch. From a purely practical standpoint, if most of your driving is in the city, why bother with a gearshift, especially in an area calling for stop-and-go driving on steep hills? On the other hand, if you rarely drive downtown, you could probably expect to save a *little* fuel with a five-speed.

There are some rational pros and cons to both automatic and manual transmissions, but it comes down to a matter of personal choice. Some folks just like to shift gears; it gives them something to do. But this is a distinctly personal decision.

The bottom line is that automatics have become extremely dependable and cause an insignificant reduction in gas mileage.

TILT WHEEL. If two drivers of different sizes share the car, a tilt wheel is more than just a luxury. The tilt wheel, along with an adjustable seat-back, is especially nice for varying your driving position on long drives. These "comfort" extras can be real life-savers for handicapped individuals, people with back problems, and anyone of unusual proportions. The nice thing about buying a used car is that a lot of them have all these spendy options, but they really don't add anything to the cost of the car. On a used car, they're basically free.

CRUISE CONTROL. Again, a wonderful strain-saver for long trips. It frees your right foot to move around, lessening driver fatigue. Cruise control also does a better job of holding a steady throttle setting than most drivers can, resulting in a slight increase in mileage.

Another of its virtues is the elimination of "itchy-foot syndrome." Just set the cruise to the speed of ambient traffic, put on some nice, mellow music, and go with the flow. For some reason, the urge to "go just a little faster" doesn't seem to happen when your foot isn't on the gas pedal all the time!

The first cruise control I ever owned was in a big, comfortable Oldsmobile I used for the same hundred-mile, all-highway drive to the auction every week. I tried to be conscientious about maintaining the speed limit, but when riding along in a big, quiet car with the stereo playing, the speed always started creeping up. So, after the second speeding ticket in a year, I installed cruise control and ended the problem. It's a genuine convenience to set your speed and let the wonderful little electronic gadget hold it there for you. One speeding ticket will pay for it, too.

POWER WINDOWS. Pure decadent luxury? There

are two valid reasons for power windows. The first may sound trivial, but for a long-legged driver it's nice *not* to have that always-in-the-wrong-place window crank banging your knee.

The second reason is that power windows give you control of all of the windows in the car. No more problems with somebody rolling down the back window when you have the air conditioning on, either. Most power-window systems have a lock button on the driver's panel. It disables all the window controls except for yours. Also, you can open the right-side window without stretching all the way across the car. Power windows are dependable and in anything like normal use, give no more problems than do regular crank-up windows.

POWER DOOR LOCKS. This is another luxury that's real easy to get used to; particularly in a four-door, or even a full-size two-door that's difficult to reach across. When you are alone with the car, your door-lock controls all doors simultaneously. Again, a dependable option worth having. Another freebie on a used car!

POWER MIRRORS. Have you ever needed to adjust your right mirror as you were motoring down the highway? Power mirrors let you do it with ease. These are yet another used-car bonus found on a lot of high-end domestic and foreign cars. No problems, either. They are even more dependable than the manual remote-control mirrors whose long, circuitous cables often fail.

POWER SEATS. One of the best features of most power seats is the range of adjustment not possible with a manual seat. A deluxe power seat will go up, down, back and forth; the front and back of the seat can be raised independently of each other, yielding an infinite range of tilt angles; and the backrest angle is independently adjustable, too. Add a tilt-wheel, and you've got comfort.

There are very few defective power-seat mechanisms. The only ones I've seen were on older GM cars that had not seen the best of care. Run all power seats through every range of travel while test-driving a prospective car. Make sure that the seats go up and down evenly, without one side going faster or farther than the other, resulting in a leaning seat.

When looking over a prospective car, don't assume that because the driver's seat is powered that the passenger's seat is also powered. Lots of cars have a power seat on the driver's side only. The tilting backrest is an option independent from the power seat.

Power seats are great if you're short, too. Most power seats have an up-and-down range that allows you to raise the seat way higher than the fixed height of a non-power seat. No more being barely able to see over the dash panel! A nice safety feature.

SPLIT BENCH SEAT. Again, a wonderful convenience for drivers of different sizes. If you're five-one and you would still like to leave some legroom for your right-seat passenger, a split bench seat makes it possible. And if you're tall, there will still be room in back for someone sitting behind your front-seat passenger. Of course, individual or bucket seats will accomplish this as well, but the option of three-across seating in front is lost. Another item of personal choice.

REAR DEFROST. This option is redundant if you have air-conditioning and learn how to use it to keep the windows clear on the inside (See Air Conditioning, below). Without A/C, a rear defroster is great in almost any climate. Ends forever not being able to see through a fogged-up rear window. Since a rear defrost system consists of nothing more than an electrically-heated piece of glass, it is totally dependable and maintenance-free. You do need to be careful when cleaning the window, however. Very thin wires are "printed" on the inside of the glass and can be damaged with ice scrapers or scouring pads. Best to use glass cleaner and a soft cloth.

HIGH-DOLLAR FACTORY STEREOS. If you happen to get one for no extra charge on a used car, fine. However, *never* pay extra for any kind of a fancy factory radio on a used car.

Bear in mind that for about $300, you can buy a really dynamite aftermarket, high-powered, full-featured stereo from any of hundreds of discount sound-equipment stores. Many such stores can install the equipment they sell, too.

This entire argument presumes that you want a good sound system in your car. If you find the sound of the radio already in your car satisfactory, leave it alone. But if you desire high-quality sound equipment, don't expect to get it from a factory radio. Some of the really expensive factory-optional radios sound pretty good if you don't turn them up too high, but they are always more expensive than a far superior aftermarket system would be. The exception to this is in cars from about '94 on up. The automakers finally figured out that they were missing an opportunity by not offering really high-quality sounds, so they're getting better and better. It's still less expensive to go with an aftermarket system, though.

AIR CONDITIONING. If I *had to* choose between a beat-up, twenty-year-old clunker with air and a brand new, high-dollar cruiser without it, you can bet I'd take the clunker. With air, you have complete control of the climate in your car at all times.

Everyone knows the benefits of air-conditioning on hot days; passengers and driver arrive at destinations refreshed rather than sweaty and rumpled. But very few people know that air works well in cold and/or humid weather as well. Most people equate air-conditioning with "cold." Try equating air-conditioning with "humidity-control" and it will become a much more useful tool.

For years, I lived on the Oregon coast. The temperature was rarely above 70 degrees, and it rained a lot. I used the air-condition all the time, and especially on cool, rainy days.

Ever get into your car on a cool morning, especially with a few other people, and have all the windows fog up instantly? Just turn on the air, set the temperature at a comfortable level, and the windows will clear up and stay that way. And it's almost instant! How this works is that the air-conditioner passes the nice, dry, dehumidified cold air through the heater-core. The result is dry, warm air that immediately removes the moisture from the insides of the windows. It works much faster than the defroster. Actually, many late-model cars now automatically turn on the A/C when you switch on the defroster, giving the same effect.

If you live where your windows often fog up on the inside, A/C can be considered an essential safety feature.

There are myths afloat about air conditioning requiring five or ten horsepower to operate, dropping gas mileage by several miles per gallon. Again, *not true!* A one or two mile-per-gallon penalty can be expected, depending on the car. Generally, the bigger the car, the less significant, percentage-wise, the drop will be.

But check this out: an interesting comparison is that running your A/C creates about the same drop in gas mileage as the extra wind-drag from driving with your windows down. Take your pick!

The only costs of having and operating an air-conditioner are a slight decrease in gas mileage, and the minor inconvenience to whomever services your car: things are a bit more cramped in the engine compartment with the compressor in the way.

Air-conditioning compressors are very reliable and can be expected to perform without a hitch to about 100,000 miles, at which time many will need a rebuild.

It is *essential* to operate the air-conditioning system frequently (at least a half-hour per month) to keep the seals from drying out and subsequently leaking.

Options: get 'em all!

By now, it may seem that I advise getting every option available. Well, just about. What I advise is getting every option that is of interest to *you*. Options are just one of the excellent reasons to buy a pre-owned car. Let somebody else pay for all the extras! In the used-car market, most of the options cost very little extra. If you tend to replace your car every few years, you will find that a car without some options--especially air--can be difficult to sell, unless you are willing to let it go for less than market price. The newer the car, the worse the penalty.

On cars older than about five years, it's a buyer's market. Not even the infamous "book" shows a value increase for options in the older cars. The older the car, the less extra you'll have to pay for the extras.

Safety Issues

There's more and more media hype about safety issues, and most car manufacturers use safety as a big selling point. My take is that we've maybe gone far enough, if not too far.

Many years ago, we had driver training programs that taught skillful and defensive driving techniques. Nowadays, if you can steer a car around the block and get it back into the lot in one piece, you've got your license. You can miss the most important questions on the written test and still pass. Why, if everyone is truly concerned about safety, is nobody concerned about knowing how to drive?

There's more to driving than being able to steer a car. In my million-plus miles of driving, I've avoided a number of death-defying accidents by using some basic defensive driving techniques. Take rear-end collisions, for example. In the first place, it's safe to say that just about every rear-end collision is caused by following too closely behind the car in front. Had there been adequate room, there would have been no collision. OK, so what if you're doing the unthinkable and actually following too close, and the guy in front slams on his brakes with no warning? Most people react by slamming on their brakes, right?

When you slam on your brakes in an emergency situation like that, the likelihood is great that you will skid the tires. Skidding tires are all but useless in stopping a car, especially if the pavement is anything but clean and dry. Your first reaction should be to look for an escape route.

In most situations when somebody in front of you slams on the brakes, there's room on the shoulder to pull safely up along side of them. That gives you plenty of room to stop. What if the shoulder is narrow and you might run into some shrubbery, or worse yet a ditch? What's worse, running into a ditch and possibly doing some minor damage to your car, or slamming into the back of another car and certainly doing a lot of damage to both cars, plus possibly causing some injuries?

Next time you find yourself in traffic, keep this topic in mind and see how it looks in real life.

OK, back to the safety issues. The car companies now devote most of their advertising to telling you how you can be totally careless with their cars. You can crash into walls, not watch where you're going, and just be generally irresponsible, because nothing will happen to you when you crash the car. Each year, there are more "safety features" on our cars, and each year the cars get more expensive. Where will it stop? Maybe when we fill the whole car with airbags and inflate them even before we drive away.

Anti-locking brakes are a good case in point. Tests have shown that these ultra-complex, computer-controlled systems offer no advantage at all, unless the driver slams the brakes to the floor and keeps the pedal there. In other words, they offer no advantage to a competent driver. What they do accomplish is to inflate the price of the car, and make sure that only a high-tech shop with the latest, sophisticated equipment can service them, again costing the consumer more money. There is no substitute for driver-skill, and all the so-called idiot-proof equipment in the world will never replace it.

It's amazing how many cars are still on the road with no air bags, anti-locking brakes or any of the other highly praised safety-equipment that we all consider essential now.

"Hi-milers"

How about those cars with lots of miles on them? What about the popular notion that a car is "worn out" when the odometer reaches 100,000 miles?

Well, here's another story. A few years ago, I drove an amazingly loose mid-size Chevy with only twenty-thousand miles on it. It rattled everywhere even on fairly smooth roads, and its rough-running engine was way too noisy. The car had belonged to a woman who lived on a ranch in eastern Oregon. It was her job to deliver lunches to the men working out in the fields, and she used the car for those deliveries. (There were no roads in the fields!)

Her car appeared to never have been serviced. It had the original oil filter (and oil?) in the engine.

There was no filter element in the dust-packed air cleaner. The air cleaner element had apparently become so clogged with dust that it had been discarded and never replaced.

Compared to another car of the same make, model and year that had been used primarily on long highway trips, and had been properly serviced at regular intervals for 100,000 miles, which do you think is the better car?

A savvy shopper needs to check closely because a professional detail and service job can make a car like that Chevy above, appear to be in good shape.

The good news is that since most people truly believe the high-miles-worn-out myth, excellent high-mile cars can usually be bought so cheaply that even if you do have to do a major repair in a year or two, you're still way ahead.

I have sold a number of carefully-selected high-milers to friends who trusted me and believed what I just told you, and I've received back nothing but glowing reports of appreciation for the bargains. Not once has anyone to whom I sold a high-miler come back with any regrets.

High-milers, up to about three years old, are the most dramatic dollar-savers. And let's face it, a two-year-old car with ninety thousand miles on the odometer can't have seen a lot of city driving. Straight, constant-speed highway miles just don't wear out a car very fast.

For example, if you have to drive the 400 miles from San Francisco to L.A., your transmission has to shift through the gears (which is what eventually wears out any transmission) about as many times as when you drive five miles across town to go shopping. I use the transmission as an obvious example, but there are literally hundreds of wearing parts in any vehicle, and the most wear is produced in stop-and-go driving.

This is exactly why a late-model, super-clean high-miler is generally an excellent choice. It's a pretty safe bet that any car that has logged thirty thousand or more miles per year has seen highway miles almost exclusively. Such cars are often offered for sale by the companies whose own employees have logged the miles, in which case service records are usually available, too. Check your classifieds for late-model cars listed as having high miles.

Don't ever believe that high-mileage car is necessarily a worn-out car. Lots of cars with over 100,000 miles on them are good for at least another 50,000 miles before needing any major repairs, and the really well-maintained ones will do a lot better than that.

Of course, the obvious exception to the above would be a car that's been used in constant, daily delivery service. But in this case, the wear-and-tear would be obvious

The high-miler is an especially great value for the person who doesn't drive all that much. Like, if you only drive five- or ten-thousand miles a year, and you buy a like-new car with 100,000 miles on it, you can expect at least another five years of use out of that car before you need to spend a dime on it for repairs.

In sparsely-populated parts of the country, a much higher percentage of the available used cars will be all-highway high-milers. This is simply because it is often a long way to anywhere in rural areas.

There's an exception to the "buy rural" theory, though. If you're in the market for a 4X4 or other kind of work/utility vehicle, it's often best to find these in the cities. Back-country trucks, especially 4X4's, tend to have been run hard all their lives. The city 4X4's are often bought as lifestyle symbols and rarely leave the pavement.

And remember, if you're looking for an older car, use the same inspection and evaluation guidelines as for a newer one.

Summary

It might seem that "deciding what you need" is pretty elementary, but there are lots of little considerations that are worth checking into *before* you go out and buy that car.

Better gas mileage is rarely a valid reason for changing cars. The arithmetic is easy to do if you'd like to determine whether or not gas-savings justify the expense of a new car.

If you would really like a bigger car for its safety and comfort, but the gas mileage factor is dictating a smaller one, there are some easy ways to drive the bigger car for less money.

Older cars in excellent condition are often the best values of all. They're built to last, comfortable, inexpensive to buy, cheaper to maintain, repair, and insure. Owning an older car also allows you to sidestep the biggest cost of most people's car-ownership: depreciation.

If you're partial to American cars, or would never buy anything other than a Japanese car, you might want to do some research before you assume that the Toyota you like is actually made in Japan, or that your favorite Chevy is made in the United States!

You like lots of optional extras? Go for all you can get, and never mind all the stories you've heard about how unreliable or costly they are. Power options are generally as dependable as their non-power equivalents, and unlike the popular myth, power steering or air-conditioning really don't make a significant difference in gas mileage!

Immaculate cars with lots of miles on them are often the best buys of all. A late-model car with 100,000 well-maintained highway miles on it is often in far better shape than another car that's been driven 40,000 miles in the city and with minimal maintenance. Don't let the myth about a car being worn out when the odometer hits 100,000 miles stop you from taking advantage of a real bargain!

GOING IN PREPARED
A Couple of Stories

Old lessons are sometimes well remembered. Throughout this chapter, I would like to share with you some experiences from a sales position I held (ages ago) for the sole purpose of learning the inside story of how a big dealership worked. Their methods haven't changed.

Many of this dealer's customers were young couples who already owned, free and clear, an older but dependable car. One such couple had talked themselves into shopping for a new car because rising fuel prices had made their old ride with its poor gas mileage too expensive to run. On that rationale, they justified a new car.

They were run through the system and saddled with a debt load far beyond their budget. The interest payments alone on their newly-acquired debt would have paid for *all* the gas for their old, paid-for car. But they did drive away in a shiny new ride. (New to them; this was a used-car dealer.)

They soon realized that with their new baby, they could no longer afford the payments, but they owed way more on their car than they could possibly sell it for. What were their options?

They could have gotten a high-interest, finance-company loan to pay the difference between what they could sell the car for and what they owed on it; but that would have meant making payments to a finance company for a car they no longer owned. Or they could have let it be repossessed and ruin their hard-earned credit rating. They were in a serious bind.

If they had not been *sold* more car than they needed, they would have avoided the whole dilemma. *Their* needs weren't even considered by the sales staff.

Jean, a bright, young woman feeling particularly good about her new job, decided that she now needed a newer car. She spent many hours pondering her decision and worked hard to narrow the selection, and especially to keep it within her budget. Then she went to a slick dealer who talked her into buying a *brand-new* car for way over her "firm" dollar limit. Sounds preposterous, doesn't it?

It happens all the time, and it happened to Jean because she went shopping unprepared for the assault on her sensibilities that she encountered in the candy-store atmosphere of the showroom.

Disclaimer

Let's take a break here. Before you read the rest of this chapter, I should tell you something. I've passed this same information on to a number of women friends and acquaintances over the years, and it's amazing what varied responses it brings. Some listen and take it to heart. They probably think I'm exaggerating a little to make a point (I'm not!), but they still listen. And when they're out there in the reality of car-shopping, they put what they've heard to use and cut a great bargain on a good car, and even enjoy doing it.

Others have told me that I should just butt out, keep this kind of depressing stuff to myself, and not ruin their fun. They tell me that they only buy a car once every few years, always trade in the old one, and always get a great deal. And then to prove their point, they'll even show me the new car they bought and give me the numbers. Well, I don't like to say "I told you so," so I keep my mouth shut. I don't tell them that they just spent a thousand dollars they didn't need to, and I don't show them any of the obvious things wrong with the new car. To some, shopping for a car is a fun-filled, emotionally-charged event, and *it's worth the extra money* to go into it blind and just go with the exhilaration. I have no quarrel with that philosophy, especially with those who can afford it. I'm addressing those women who are serious about getting the most value for their hard-earned dollars. Hey, that can be a fun-filled, emotionally-charged event in itself!

So if you enjoy going along with the normal process of car-buying and feel comfortable with spending a lot of money you might have been able to use better elsewhere, you might just want to skip the rest of this chapter. It *explains* the normal process of car-buying, and it's often not a pretty picture.

How it Works

Even the sanest, most rational, most conservative person has difficulty keeping emotions out of the decision to buy a car. Few people can buy a car without visualizing themselves driving up somewhere: "What does this car say about me?" (You're lucky; women have it a little easier making rational car-decisions, because they don't have to deal with the testosterone thing.)

Americans, men and women, identify with their "wheels," some more than others. Some are hard-pressed to admit it, but even the most reluctant will concede that it feels better to drive a nice-looking car than a clunker.

Every salesman knows this, and lives and breathes its importance.

The auto-salesman's creed: "When you buy a car you're not merely buying transportation. You are buying a lifestyle."

Almost all auto purchases are emotional decisions. Just take a look at the ads! How do car makers advertise their products? Do they tell you how good their cars are? Do they give you any specifications or other details to demonstrate their worth? Nowadays, as close as they get is to tell you how crash-proof their cars are, and anything they say they've done beyond what's required by Federal standards is mostly hype.

What they *do* tell you is how good that car is going to make you *feel*. They show you how much sex appeal you'll generate by being associated with their merchandise. Or if you happen to belong to a different demographic group, they'll show you how you can one-up your business associates with their flashier-than- last-year's model.

Not that there's anything at all wrong with having your new car make you feel good. There's real value in that, for sure, and it can be worth real money to you. The key here is to *recognize the difference* between the buying-motivation for feel-good reasons, and a buying motivation for practical reasons. This is essential for you to stay in control during the purchasing process.

There needn't be anything wrong with letting emotions play a part in the car-selection process. But you've got to recognize the emotional pull--and control it. Not recognizing your emotional involvement is dangerous because it allows the professional, highly-trained salesman to get the upper hand . . . and keep it.

Sales people are actually taught that emotion is the most powerful sales tool in their bag. The necessity to direct the buyer's emotions is why the most successful salesmen may know more about psychology than they do about automobiles.

Most dealers actually prefer that their sales people be basically auto-illiterate. Knowing a lot about the product just gets in the way of selling it; a good salesman doesn't sell the product, he sells himself. These words, by the way, are not mine. They are highlighted in nearly every sales manual in every field.

And when I speak of "salesmen," I refer to women as well. Women are often very effective in auto sales. Some auto-sales seminar speakers even address the specific potentials a good-looking woman has in selling vehicles to men.

I know one woman who has a great deal of fun selling four-wheel-drive rigs to *men*. The more macho the guy, the more fun she has, and the greater the likelihood of a sale. She's an expert at manipulation and intimidation, and she loves her work!

This same woman, and I don't believe she's alone, also effectively uses a perceived "sisterhood" as a confidence-builder when selling to other women. Her goal is to sell cars, and she's good at it.

The Mind-Games

Most car buyers have few, if any, guidelines to follow when they enter the marketplace. First and foremost, *knowing and believing* that buying a car is rarely a rational decision is the foundation for making an intelligent automobile purchase. The salesman knows it, and he puts it to work when he first sees you enter the lot.

When a salesman asks you your name, he really isn't just trying to be friendly; he's starting the well-calculated game of control. He will ask your name and use it often to convince you that he cares about you. And of course, he also *really* cares about your family, your needs, and whatever else he senses might push your buttons. But it's all just part of the carefully-designed system that has evolved into a most effective mind-control game. Once rapport is established, it gets a lot easier to lead the customer to whatever conclusion the salesman likes.

Sorry if this sounds a little cynical. For sure, there are auto salespeople who really do care about you and are there to make sure you have a nice day, if not a good deal on a car. I've even known dealers who will try to talk a customer *out* of buying a car that looks to be a budget-breaker. But they are few and far between. It is *not* good business to assume that your salesperson is one of the good guys.

Most professional car salespeople, particularly the ones working in franchised dealers' stores (and even *more* particularly in the big-city locations), are intensively trained in this system. They will keep nodding at you to encourage a positive response; they know that purchases are based on *feelings*, not on product quality, nor on price. They'll ask carefully-phrased questions that can only be answered positively, furthering the *yes* that they'll need at the "close" of the sale.

A seasoned professional will continue to "sell the car" by relating its positive points to the personal clues that you give him. For example, if you have four children and your primary concern is safety, he will show you statistics that point out the "crash protection" offered by whatever he's trying to sell you. If your opening remarks concern economy, he'll go off about the terrific mileage of the same car. If you let him know you have a respiratory problem, the car he's showing you will have a special dust filter in the air-conditioning. *All of these sales ploys will be freely offered whether or not the salesman has a clue as to what he's talking about.*

And to most sales people, telling you what you want to hear, whether or not it's true, is perfectly OK. It's even encouraged by most sales managers, and as you'll see in Chapter 9, "The FTC Sticker," Federal law says that it's quite alright for the salesman to lie to you, as long as he doesn't put it in writing (believe it or not!). For the most part, you're much better off to just make your own evaluations, and disregard everything you hear from the sales staff. If you still don't entirely trust your own evaluations, even after reading this book, take along someone who you can depend on to help out.

It's a Control Thing

Rarely will you be offered the positive features of two or more cars so that you can make your own decision. A well-trained salesman will not relinquish that much control to his "mark" (as the customer is called in some training seminars). The salesman is programmed to know that if he sells himself, the customer will *trust* his information and guidance. Even if later, the car turns out to be a lemon, the salesman is not likely to be blamed.

Here's an abbreviated outline of techniques taken directly from sales seminars:

1. Greet the customer warmly when s/he enters the showroom.

2. Give a hearty "welcome" with a friendly handshake to put her at ease.

3. Establish control. Phrase questions very carefully to remove the option of saying, "No," or, "Just looking."

4. Get on a first name basis and use that name often in conversation.

5. Give a business card so the customer can recall your name. It puts the customer at ease if s/he doesn't have to fret about forgetting the name of such a swell guy.

6. Work the "hinge": keep nodding to encourage agreement.

7. Offer premature "Congratulations" to instill the idea of ownership.

8. And even this: Pay careful attention to smoking: smoke if s/he does, don't if s/he doesn't.

The salesman works to discover your main reason for wanting to buy a car, and he asks specific questions to discover that reason. He has been trained to know how to work his customer from that standpoint.

Finding which of your buttons to push is his immediate goal, and there are some really effective routines in the training manuals for just that purpose. (There are also some really effective techniques in this book to make certain that *you* stay in control!)

He phrases his questions very carefully, always assuming that you, the buyer, are already sold. You'll rarely hear a question that can be answered with a "yes" or a "no." Even that much control is not allowed the customer.

"Why are you looking for a new car today?" If you tell him directly, he will know directly where to steer you to make his sell most effective.

"Who's the new car going to be for?" The clever salesman already has you thinking about the person(s) you will be disappointing if you don't go through with this purchase.

"Where will you be taking your first trip in your new car?"

Now you'll be thinking about showing up at Margie's in that new ride. Note the part about " . . . *your* new car." It's already yours, right?

"Who else will be proud of the fact that you now own this car?"

Talk about presumptuous! In the first place, you don't own it yet. Secondly, the salesman is assuming that you are buying a car to make you proud. "Who else will be proud" is to set you to thinking of all of the people you will impress with your new car. This simple technique actually works well enough on some folks to close the sale right there!

"Is this car going to be for a special occasion--an anniversary or a birthday?--or are you just rewarding yourself?"

The salesman is making it ever more difficult for you to tell him that you might not even buy today.

We'll cover the techniques you can use to stay in control while all this is going on, but the starting point is always to be very clear on what you're shopping for before you even talk with any sales people. A salesman's goal is to make a sale, and to that end, he'll tell you *anything* he thinks you want to hear.

The "Turn-Over" System

The dealership where I got the first-hand experience mentioned above was what is known as a "T-O House." "T-O" stands for turn-over, the name of the sales-system. This system, or variations of it, are used in most large dealerships nation-wide. Here is a simplified description of the basics. Please remember that although the names are fictitious, the story is true.

When Barbara came on the lot, Harvey approached her with his well-rehearsed pitch. If for any reason--maybe she didn't like his haircut, or his style of speech--he felt that he was no longer in control of the conversation, he turned her over to George, who just happened to be standing inconspicuously nearby (as a part of the system). By turning over the deal, Harvey had also split the commission, should George make a sale.

If George also found himself losing control of his customer, he again turned her over to strategically-placed John. The commission would take another split. The turn-over would go something like this: "Gee, Barbara, I'm not sure I can answer that question, but let me introduce you to John here.

That's his field, and he can help you with that." And then George silently vanishes. This would go on until finally one of the salesmen could relate to Barbara.

With this dealer, it was standard practice, and still is in many dealerships, to con the customer out of the keys to her car immediately after getting her into the "box" (the little sales cubicles in most dealerships). Getting a customer's car keys was incredibly easy: "Our appraiser is here, so let's just have him check out your car and get that out of the way."

Why did they want the keys? The keys are one of the most effective controls in the business. Example: The customer is in the box. She'd been there for five hours and six different salesmen had each done their best but had still not closed a deal. She was frazzled, after dealing with each salesman's spiel, and the piles of paperwork.

John, the last salesman, had Barbara fill out a long, involved form which stated that she promised that she would, in fact, buy the car if the terms could be made to her approval. John said that he didn't dare bring in such a low offer to his boss (the sales manager, who usually hides in a back office) without having a promise that the customer wasn't just window shopping. Of course his boss, Harold, had been listening in the whole time over the intercom system which was hidden in each box, so he knew exactly what was going on.

But John was now losing what control he still had over his customer. At just the right time, Harold came in and told John that his mother was on the phone and it sounded pretty important. That was the salesman's standard cue to get lost. Then Harold would start in on the poor customer. Harold was a real pro. Nobody walked on the boss.

Harold would probably close the sale in a short time, but if he had any trouble, if his exasperated customer got really mad and said she was just going to walk out, the boss would put on his best surprised look and tell her, with a straight face, that he didn't understand. "Walk out? Why we've already wholesaled your car. . . . remember that form you signed? You authorized us to wholesale your car. You don't *have* a car any more, lady."

Of course, he hadn't really wholesaled her car, that was just another lie. The car had been locked up in the warehouse kept for just this purpose down the street.

Sounds hard to believe, right? Some kind of fictitious horror story. Well, believe it. It happened, and it is happening somewhere right now. Small wonder lots of people are seriously intimidated by just thinking about going car-shopping!

Another common maneuver if a deal was close at hand, was to ask the customer if there was anything about the car that needed attention: any repairs or adjustments that could be made which would make the difference. Of course, almost any customer offered a choice like that will go for it. So George breaks out this special form, the "Customer's Authorization for Repairs," and fills in all the blanks.

"Sure. Let's see now, we'll adjust the brakes, fix the radio, replace the rear tires, and straighten that little ding in the fender. Sure thing. Just sign here." He would fill out the form with all the repairs that the customer requested, have the customer sign it, and then give it to her.

What did the customer then have in hand? A worthless piece of paper with her own signature on it. Nowhere on the official-looking form was the name of the dealership. Nowhere did any representative of the dealership sign the form. It was useless, but the customer liked it. It sold the car, too.

The customer would then ask when and where these repairs were to be done. And George (and everybody else on the sales staff) was trained to say that "Fred," the house mechanic, was recovering from surgery and would be back at work in a week or two, so bring the car back then. George could make up any lie which came to mind, but the phantom mechanic's name was always Fred. Any customer query about the whereabouts of Fred was a cue to tell another lie about why Fred wasn't available just now.

Fred didn't exist. Really!

The customer would usually get tired of the game in a month or two of trying to get repairs made, and quit. On the rare occasion that a customer got wise and threatened to sue the house for the repairs, she was reminded that she had nothing saying the dealership owed her any repairs. None of the salesmen had ever seen that silly form before: "Where did that come from?"

Bizarre but True

If these stories sound bizarre, be advised that this kind of treachery goes on in some of the best-looking dealerships. I could tell you stories that make these seem tame, but their very flagrancy diminishes their credibility. The point is not to relate stories of what has happened before and is happening now at some level in many dealerships around the country. The point is to arm you with enough information so that you can *recognize and evade the traps* long before they become dangerous.

I have known more than a few reasonable, rational, intelligent adults who became victims of a highly-skilled sales staff. They were so smoothly manipulated throughout the whole operation-- obligated to an impossible contract on a car they neither needed or wanted--that when the inevitable buyer's remorse set in, they blamed partners, spouses, or friends for making "the stupid decision to buy this @%$# car."

It never occurred to them that they had been victimized by a staff of people highly trained in psychological warfare, not only highly trained in their specialized craft, but constantly retrained to keep them at their best. How can a person who only buys one car every few years hope to stand up to such a formidable opponent?

During my short stay at this dealership, the lengths gone to in selling a car were astonishing. The financial ruin laid on people naive enough to trust the salesmen was unforgivable. Some of the outright junk that was sold as "fine used cars" was unthinkable. I found the deceit, dishonesty, outright lying, and insidious mind games played with customers unbelievable, and stayed there only long enough to see how the T-O system worked.

Often, a couple would come onto the lot after work, wander around and look over the inventory with one of the salesmen in hot pursuit. And the staff, however many of them it took, would coerce them, brainwash them, argue with them, and do whatever was necessary--even if it took until two o'clock the next morning--to sell them a car.

And sell them a car they would. The mind games were so effective that if necessary, the "closer" could do something as outrageous as to skillfully maneuver them into a position in which one of them would threaten divorce if the car wasn't bought. (I saw it happen.) Or he would back the stronger of the two into a corner from which he (or she) had but two choices: either sign the contract, or admit in front of the spouse to being some kind of lowlife liar, pervert, or whatever else suited the salesman's whims at the moment. It was hard to believe that I was actually seeing this happen.

If somebody had told me about this and I hadn't seen it for myself, I'd find it hard to believe. I related some of these stories to my brother-in-law, and he didn't believe me. So I challenged him to come down and pose as a customer and allow himself to be run through the system. Armed with all the stories I had told him, he did just that. And several hours later, he had no more doubts.

OK, so it is a little depressing to know that this kind of treachery is so common. But the importance of knowing that it exists lies in your being able to recognize it. There is a common thread that runs through most of the con-games played at disreputable dealerships. Now that you've been exposed to a few of them by just safely reading about them, you should be able to recognize similar efforts right away. The safest thing to do is to leave any dealership where you feel you're being hustled. It's not like there's a scarcity of car dealers to choose from!

OK! So How Can I Beat the Game?

Sounds like a frustrating situation, doesn't it? Well, there *are* ways to deal with it. If you are shopping for a used car, you have two options: buy from a private party (see Chapter 3), or find a reasonable, reputable dealer.

Your chances of finding a dealer to work with in a climate which could still be called human relations are increased if you restrict your search to independent dealers. That clearly *excludes* the used car department of most new-car stores. Most new-car stores *have* to run each customer, each sale, through the system.

Even if you go onto the lot looking at an old Toyota which ought to sell for $1200, you will still be subjected to the same barrage of intimidation that you would meet if you were looking at a new car on the showroom floor. You will not likely get a straight answer out of anyone, about anything. Including the price of the old Toyota.

If you decide to circumvent some of the routine by asking to talk directly to the used-car sales manager, you'll first be sized-up for gullibility by the professional who greets you. He may decide to tell you that *he* is in fact the manager. Or, if he doesn't think you'll buy that, he will call the turn-over man hiding in the shadows, and introduce *him* to you as the manager you seek.

Most managers pride themselves on rarely having to lower themselves to face a "mark" (customer, in dealer-speak). A manager's inaccessibility is a direct result of the proficiency of his sales force. This is the way it works at most new-car stores, and their used-car lots. And it's all part of the system. In all fairness, however, there are exceptions.

How do you beat the game? By staying in control. By being aware of what's going on and how you, the customer, figure into it. Entering the marketplace knowing exactly what you're looking for and how much you're willing to pay for it, and knowing in advance what kinds of games the dealer is likely to play, will make you the kind of customer who can control the transaction and come out the winner.

Once you are aware of what goes on in a "T-O system house," you will recognize it if you walk into one. If you do, *immediately* tell the first salesman who comes up to you that you are just looking for your lost dog and, no, you really have no use for a car. You can't even get a driver's license because of your frequent undiagnosable fainting spells, and you can't go to another doctor because they all know about your recent bankruptcy, and has he seen your dog? No? Adios.

There *are* franchised dealerships where you can talk to someone who has the authority to sell you a car without going through a system-sell nightmare. It *is* possible in such a dealership to converse rationally with the salesperson, and to buy a vehicle without a mind-boggling bunch of red tape. The few I know of are in small towns, where repeat business becomes important. It's just easier to deal with independents.

There are also independents who utilize the same system-sell procedures. Many of these independents were trained in a new-car dealership and worked there long enough to realize that if they ran their own operation, they would no longer have to deal with management's manipulating the figures to cheat the sales staff out of most of their commissions. Yes, there's thievery within the den of thieves.

Good News!

Ready for some good news? System-house independent dealers are usually easy to recognize. First, you should be immediately suspicious of an unusually large used-car operation, particularly if there are several salesmen prowling the lot. A non-system independent usually has two sales people at most on the staff. If asked the price of a particular car, a non-system salesman will give you a direct answer, in dollars--one of the first things that the system-sell folks are taught *never* to do.

If a salesman does give a dollar figure, it will be at least $1000 over the price at which the manager (the individual salesman has no real authority) would actually sell the car. This gives the house two immediate advantages: testing the buyer's reaction and naivete and creating built-in headroom for manipulating figures when they get you in the box.

Which is not to say that the independent dealer won't highball you on the initial price. Even the most scrupulous dealer wants to get the most he can out of his merchandise and it's a lot easier to come down from a high price than to go up from a low one.

Asking around, which I so highly recommend when searching for a mechanic, cannot always be relied on when looking for a car dealer. Asking around *does* work if you get a positive referral from several different sources, especially if they all feel that they were treated well. Ask if any of these folks can relate a favorable after-the-sale story, such as the dealer taking care of a problem beyond his legal obligation. It *does* happen.

Rural communities often offer better chances to find reputable independent dealers. A real shyster will have difficulty staying in business in a small community and will certainly not be able to produce any repeat-business referrals. Most rural dealers also have less overhead than dealers in the middle of the city. Some will pass the savings onto their customers; others will only advertise that they do. Watch out for the "rural" dealer who spends zillions on TV ads telling you about the deals he can offer because of his low overhead. TV ads do not constitute "low overhead."

If you would like to do an effective research program to find referrals (don't believe them if the dealer supplies them!), find a few people sporting license frames carrying local dealers' names and ask them about the dealer where they bought their car. Grocery store parking lots are excellent for finding cars and their owners. Also ask friends, co-workers or anybody else who recently bought a car.

What About the New "Used-Car Superstores?"
There is now a trend toward used-car superstores. These are the chains, like CarMax, AutoNation, and Driver's Mart Worldwide. They are huge operations with computerized inventory and you can even look up the car and options of your choice on a video screen before meeting it in person for inspection and a test-drive. The prices are all set, much like buying a washing-machine or a blender. The pitch behind these operations is that since there is no price-haggling involved, much of the unpleasantry of car-shopping is avoided. Most of the offerings in these operations are lease and rental returns, and many are still under factory warranty. Odds are in favor of finding a well-maintained car in excellent condition. The catch is that the prices are typically higher than can be found elsewhere.

The Survival Skills

OK, armed with our new-found confidence, let's venture onto a used-car lot. The best technique to use when dealing with an auto salesman is to just pretend you are at a department store looking for an appliance you need. The appliance salesman has no need and no right to know your life history. *Neither does the car salesman!* He has no legitimate reason to ask you for any personal information whatsoever. You're in his place of business to look at merchandise he has for sale. You're *not* there to tell him about your kids, your home, or anything else personal! You ask *him* about the *car*.

If possible, start by asking a few questions to which you already know the answers (technical stuff works well, if you're into that), and see if he knows anything about the car he's selling. If you find that he knows less than you do, you've now eliminated any possible reason to talk with him about anything else.

Examine the car to your satisfaction. Bring along a knowledgeable friend and discuss it with *him or her*, not with the salesman. If the salesman insists on interjecting useless conversation in a continuing effort to work you, try your best to disregard anything he says. If that doesn't work, you can ask him to please leave you alone for a while; that you'll come find him when you need him. Some salesmen are not allowed to leave a customer unattended, and in that case you might just have to leave and try another dealer. Whatever you do, never give a salesman a straight answer to any question that seems useless or personal.

If you are uncomfortable with this technique, or if he's got exactly the car you want, you have a couple of other options. One is to simply ignore him. Pretend he isn't there. The other, which can be fun, is to answer his questions with more questions. Just keep a question ready for him at all times. If you're persistent, he'll eventually back off. The dialog might go like this:

SALESMAN: Who is this car going to be for?
YOU: What size tires does this car use?
SALESMAN: Where will you be taking your first trip?
YOU: How big is the gas tank?

Get the drift? It really is fun!

Ask anything that pops into your head. Questions that he won't be able to answer are the most effective. And fun!

Employing this technique at a T/O house will insure that you get to meet the whole staff before you leave. Maybe even the manager!

Important!!!
One of the most important self-defense tools you can have is the ability to recognize a climate in which you will be hustled. Unless you feel fully prepared to deal with it, *just walk out.* Just leave. You don't need an excuse. You owe nothing to the salesman who hustles you. You owe nothing to the dealer. You *do* owe it to yourself to get out of there at once, so do it.

More hard, fast rules:
1. Leave your checkbook at home.
2. *Never* drive your own car onto the lot.

Leave your check book at home so that you have to come back to close a deal. The deal isn't closed until the dealer has received some compensation and leaving your checkbook at home means you'll *have to* come back, giving you some time to think while away from the dealer and his sales staff.

Never believe a salesman when he tells you that this amazing offer is good "now only." He'll tell you that if you leave and come back later, you'll have to start negotiating all over again. That's the oldest line in the business and it's never true.

When you drive your car to the lot, don't even park near enough so that the sales people can see you get out of it. If the salesman knows what you drove up in, he already has an edge you don't need to give him.

If you can avoid making smalltalk with the salesman, you'll nicely derail his whole (control) agenda. He needs the feedback from the small talk to get the information that allows him to gain control. He will ask you questions and will methodically file away the answers to help him gauge your vulnerability.

Remember, you are there to look at his merchandise. *You ask the questions!* He has no legitimate need to know where you work, how much you earn, whether or not you are married, how long you have lived in the area or anything else. You've come to him to look over his inventory of goods for sale. Just keep it on that level and you'll survive.

The salesperson *will* ask about your present car. He can get valuable information about you by spending a few minutes in "friendly conversation" about the car you are now driving. Throw him another curve: tell him you don't own a car. Tell him you have been riding the bus, borrowing a car. Tell him anything, but don't tell him about your car. You are not going to trade it in (See Chapter 6, "Trade-ins"), so there is no legitimate reason for him to ask you about it and there's even less reason for you to *tell* him about it!

If you just can't fib to this person who is so willing to lie to you, then simply tell him that your present car will not be a part of this transaction, so you see no reason to discuss it. He will then give you several plausible-sounding reasons why you *should* discuss it, so you will eventually have to tell him to chill out. Or something to that effect.

But what if you're determined to buy a new car? If you are, I'd like to suggest you read the rest of this book before making that decision. But just in case . . .

Just like with a used car, before actually talking numbers with a dealer, you should already be firm about the make and model of car you want. There are a couple of good ways to make this determination without having to test-drive a dealer's car. (See Chapter 1.) Avoiding the dealer's test-drive not only keeps you away from the salesman's brainwashing efforts, but it allows you more relaxed time to get the feel of the prospective new car.

Rent your Test Drive

Probably the best way to thoroughly evaluate a car to see how you might like living with it is to rent your prospective choice for a day or two. Like from Avis or Budget. You won't find every car made in the rental fleet, but most American cars and many imports are represented. Then you can drive it where and how you wish, with nobody looking over your shoulder. The longer your test drive, the better. Go for a hundred-mile drive so that you really get a feel for the car. Take it shopping. Take the kids for a ride. Take it on a date. I've talked several people into doing this, and although they balked at the thought of paying $50/day for a test-drive, some ended up *not* buying the car of their dreams after living with it for a couple of days.

If you're thinking that a rental car might not be a viable example because they often get thrashed by careless drivers, I haven't found that to be the case. Surely, there are people who will abuse a rental car just because it isn't their own, but I believe they are a small minority. And besides, if your nearly-new rental car is already showing signs of falling apart just because of a little careless driving, there might be a message in that about the car's durability.

Another possibility is to ask a friend who owns a car like the one you're interested in to take it for a drive. And another good appraisal is going to a used-car lot and driving a high-mile example of the new car you're interested in. This will give you a good idea of what your new car might feel/look like a year or two down the road. And since you have no interest in actually buying the high-mile car, you'll be immune to the rantings of the salesman.

If you really, really want to do this new-car thing, go to a new-car dealer and test drive the model you want. But you *will* be hustled. You will be pitting your strength and will against those of the highly-trained con-men (and women) I spoke of earlier. You *must* keep your guard up at all times or you just might end up buying something you either don't want or is way over your budget. Or both.

Every attempt will be made to sell you something from that dealer's inventory and to keep you from looking elsewhere. You will be told, "You said you wanted a light blue, mid-sized two-door with an automatic, power steering and windows, and that it would have to get thirty miles per gallon on the road. This car fills those requirements perfectly. Now you say you want to go look at some other makes. You really don't know what you are looking for, do you? You told me that you knew exactly what you wanted and this car is exactly what you described. How are you going to get any closer to your needs than this?"

You will be leaned on, coerced, intimidated, and made to feel obligated to buy a car from him after he has spent so much time with you.

This is where that friend will come in handy; the one who can stand back and observe without getting emotionally involved, until it becomes necessary to get emotional in your defense! The salesman won't like it much, but that's his problem.

Walk away from the dealership if you feel like you're getting cornered, or even if you feel at all uncomfortable. Just say you need a break, and then *take it!* You can always come back if that's what you want to do.

Summary

A well-informed consumer is difficult to fool. Buying a car is, for most people, a major expense, and for the people who end up with a lemon or even a bad deal on an otherwise OK car, it can be a debilitating expense.

The most important things to remember:

1. When you go shopping, be very clear on what it is you're looking for and how much you're willing to pay for it. Take a friend along. If you have any doubts about your own car-savvy, make it somebody you can lean on, if necessary.
2. Don't get involved in personal conversation with the salesman. Keep the conversation specific to the topic at hand--buying this car.
3. Leave your checkbook at home! Having to come back gives you some valuable time away from the hustle to re-consider a deal.

4. Never consider trading in your old car. (See Chapter 6.)

5. If you feel like you're getting hustled or are no longer in control of the situation, leave!

6. Ask friends and co-workers for referrals. When you get several for the same dealer, that's the one to try.

7. See Chapter 3, "Private Party Sales," for more related info.

PRIVATE-PARTY SALES

One way to avoid dealer-induced trauma is to buy your car from a private party. This can be a pleasant experience mutually beneficial to both seller and buyer. You can even meet some interesting people! It can also be a real bummer. Here's how to make it work for you.

Most people who sell their own cars are doing exactly that: selling their own cars, (maybe even as a result of having read this book). But there are also "curbstoners," who *pose* as owners selling their own cars.

Curbstoners

Curbstoners make a living buying and selling cars without benefit of a dealer's license. There are actually so many curbstoners at work that some newspapers keep close tabs on all classified car sales in an effort to weed them out. A computer has no difficulty finding them: their phone numbers keep coming up again and again. Although it is probably unfair to the few who try their best to treat their unsuspecting customers fairly, I believe that there are so few that it is a safe recommendation to walk away from almost any transaction when it becomes clear that you are dealing with a curbstoner. I'll explain the "almost" below.

A lot of these shade-tree car dealers obtain their merchandise by buying the not-fit-for-sale trade-ins from legitimate dealers. They'll then repair what is absolutely necessary to get the car to run, disguise any other problems to the best of their abilities, clean the car enough to make it presentable and then advertise it for sale as if it were their own car, often telling some creative stories about its history.

While there is nothing at all wrong with an automobile which has been properly repaired (more on this later), there is often a *lot* wrong with the so-called rebuilt cars being sold by curbstoners who will not be around tomorrow to answer your questions.

Where do the backyard rebuilders get their merchandise? Many auto-salvage dealers (wrecking yards) make a practice of selling "rebuildables," wrecked cars which they bought at insurance salvage auctions. They're often listed as "rebuildables" in newspaper classifieds. (See Chapter 11, "Insurance.")

Some of these cars do fall into the hands of competent shop-owners who have the expertise, equipment and desire to do a proper repair job. Many do not. Most questionable rebuilds are easily detected by using the guidelines in Chapters 14 and 15.

How to Spot a "Curbstoner"

How do you identify a curbstoner? One way is when you call on an ad, and a seller tells you that his house is hard to find and he'll meet you at the local 7-11 parking lot. This one is common enough that it should send up a Big Red Flag. His house would actually be real easy to find; it's the one that looks like a used car lot!

Some will invite you to come right to their home, and they're careless enough to have several cars around which appear to belong at the same residence. Ask, "Are any of these other cars yours, too?" If the answer is yes, chances are good they haven't been his for long. More than likely, you'll get some kind of fidgety non-answer to your question. Some curbstoners are more careful and will make a point of removing any other cars so that it appears the one for sale is legitimate. One thing to check when you first see the car is the date on the license-plate sticker.

If your state issues license-plate stickers that display the *month and year* of expiration, it is easy to tell when the sticker was issued. If it was within the last month or so, keep this information in mind when you listen to the seller's story about how long he has owned the car. Possibly, even though the seller has the title and it is in his name, he registered it for the sole purpose of disguising the fact that he only recently acquired the car.

If your conversation leads you to believe that you are dealing with a curbstoner, ask him whether or not he has the title to the car. If he says that he does, ask him if it is in his name. If it is not, ask him who owns the car. If he says *he* does, ask him why the car is not registered to him.

If the transaction progresses to the point where you are shown the title of the car, observe the date when it was issued. Again, if it was in the last month or two, how does this check out with the seller's story of how long he's owned the car? Remember to ask questions; there is still time to walk away.

Another reason to examine the expiration date on the plates is to be aware of an upcoming renewal fee.

Since almost nobody ever asks these questions, unless they're a real pro, he will by now have become noticeably uneasy with your line of questioning. This may be a good time to say, "Thank you for your time," and then leave. His is not the only car for sale.

There are also enterprising curbstoners who make a good living by watching the local classified advertising weeklies and being the first in line to call on any car which appears to be priced too low. They buy all of the clearly underpriced cars they can get their hands on, then turn around and re-advertise them at a substantial profit in the regular newspaper Sunday classifieds.

These curbstoners do not buy junk and doctor it up for resale. They rely on their constant attention to market values, and make their profit by taking advantage of the probability that most people looking for a car in the classifieds can't drop everything moments after the paper hits the newsstand. They can and do, and that's what "entrepreneur" means. You can get a decent car from these people, but they won't know anything about the history of it and you might be paying too much. Again, know what you're looking for and how much it's worth to you before talking price with a seller. If the seller bought the car for a low enough price, you might still be able to buy it for your price. That happens a lot.

You've Found a Legitimate Seller

Most sellers are legitimately just trying to sell their own cars. There are many distinct advantages in buying a car from its owner, especially from its original owner, or at least from someone who has owned it for the last few years. The price will almost always be much less than at a dealership, and most owners will be able to furnish you with a history of the car's performance, maintenance, and repairs. Often the original owner has receipts for everything that has ever been done to the car.

Many people feel that they are safer buying from a dealer because the private-party seller will not guarantee the car. See Chapter 10, "Warranties," to explore this myth.

If you're real lucky, you will come across a *woman* who is selling her car that she bought new. Most women's cars I've been familiar with have been given excellent care, and have been serviced right on schedule. Unlike a lot of men, most women don't assume that their cars will run forever with no maintenance. My experience suggests that women are usually a lot easier on their cars, too. Of course, there *are* exceptions . . .

The one-on-one atmosphere of many private-party auto sales is clearly a pleasure compared to the barrage of abuse you'll get from many dealerships. But even in a more personal climate, you need to be alert for signals which tell you that something is wrong.

Always keep in mind that *your* appraisal (or that of your mechanic) will decide the fitness of the car. If your appraisal doesn't give you the same message as the sales pitch from the seller, trust your appraisal. And any time a seller refuses to allow you to show the car to your mechanic, try somewhere else.

Of course, *you've* got to be reasonable, too. You can't expect a seller to let you take the car to a mechanic twenty or thirty miles away. If you don't have someone nearby to inspect the car, you should take someone along with you to check out any car that you are serious about.

If you really need to take a car farther than is comfortable with the seller, you can always leave a deposit on it, making the purchase subject to the approval of your mechanic. Be sure to get a receipt for your *refundable* deposit.

Even if you feel qualified to do the inspecting yourself, it's always a good idea to take along a friend when you go car shopping. A capable third party can often find discrepancies that you might overlook and a little moral support never hurts, either!

Wheelin' and Dealin'

The same bargaining techniques apply in dealing with private party sales as with dealers. Know what you're willing to pay before you start tossing numbers around! If the seller is asking way more than you're willing to pay, offer way less than you're willing to pay. You would be surprised at how little a lot of people will take for their cars, if you just ask! I'm still surprised occasionally, when I offer someone a ridiculously low price for a car I'm barely interested in, and they just say, "OK" without so much as a blink. Then I have to wonder how much *less* they would have taken, had I come in lower!

Don't tell the seller that what s/he has to offer is exactly what you want. Even if it is, your bargaining position will be better if you let it be known that this isn't the only one around and you're not that fond of the color, anyway.

Check all your local classifieds and even local bulletin boards. Every once in a while, you'll find a genuine, honest seller who has just what you're looking for at a reasonable price. It does happen, and it sure feels good when it does!

MILES PER GALLON vs. MILES PER DOLLAR

Ask several friends what the term "economy car" means and you'll hear mostly about gas mileage. Well, an economy car, by definition, should be economical, right? And "economical" implies that it will cost less to own and operate than one which is less economical. Gas mileage alone is not the answer.

If you are looking for an excuse to go out and spend a small fortune on a new mini-car, and you're leaning towards "better gas mileage" as the rationale, read on.

Let's use Mary Smith as an example to illustrate the entire concept of "economy car."

Mary now drives an eight-year-old Maxicruiser with a small V-8 engine, automatic transmission, power steering and air. It shows 87,000 miles on the odometer and is in better-than-average condition. It gets about 14 mpg in town and 20 on the highway.

Mary just got a new job (she's a computer programmer) and her Maxi was the only big, old car in the company parking lot. Everybody else got with the program and bought one of those new, egg-shaped mini-cars. And now Mary "needs" a new car. In her quest for reasons to replace the Maxicruiser, Mary settled on better economy.

After several trips to various new- and used-car dealers, she finally decided on a three-year-old Minicar. The new ride was equipped with a five-speed transmission, a nice stereo and air. It showed 30,000 miles on the odometer. Its price was $6995, which she skillfully negotiated down to $6000.

The dealer allowed her $1000 for her Maxicruiser against the purchase price of the Minicar.

She was given the usual choice between an "extended warranty" or signing the AS-IS clause (See Chapter 10), and she opted for the $400 "warranty." After subtracting the value of her trade-in as her down payment, and paying outright for the license/tax/transfer fees, she signed a thirty-six-month contract for a balance of a little over $5400, drove her new car home, and proudly parked it in the driveway. She now had a car just like everyone else's on the block.

Mary wasn't happy to find that her insurance premium had nearly doubled because of the new car. Her agent explained that she had carried no collision on the old Maxicruiser, but since she was financing the new car, the lender insisted she now carry collision. And as expensive as the newer cars were to repair (even a 5-mph tap on the front bumper of that Minicar could do over $1300 damage, she was told), it just wasn't bright to drive without collision, even if it wasn't required. Mary understood, but the extra $220 hurt just the same.

Since most of her driving was the commute to work--nearly all highway driving--the Minicar was getting about 33 mpg. Maybe she *could* make her payments out of what she saved on gas, as the salesman had promised.

The Numbers Tell the Story

Let's figure it out. Mary drives about 15,000 miles per year. The Maxicruiser averaged 17 mpg. 15,000 miles at 17 mpg comes to 882 gallons of fuel. At $1.50 a gallon, that's $1323.

The Minicar uses 500 gallons annually at its average of 30 mpg. That comes to $750 for a year's supply of gas. So far, Mary shows a savings of $573/year, or $47.75/month.

The added $220 for insurance coverage not needed for the old car drops her savings a bit: now she's down to about $350/year, or $29/month.

Oh, yes, car payments. $5400 for thirty-six months, financed at 11%, comes to "easy monthly payments" of only $179.36.

But she's saving $29 a month, right? Right. So for driving a car half the size, half the comfort, and a fraction of the safety when compared to the sturdy old Maxicruiser, Mary pays only $150/month *more* to drive the Minicar. Keep track of this figure for a few moments; we'll get back to it.

Figuring only principal, interest and the down payment, she will have spent a total of $7457 over the life of the contract. After three years, she'll actually begin "saving" that $17 a month because the Minicar will be paid off.

But will she be able to live with her basic Minicar for longer than three years? Won't there be sufficient reasons by then to justify another new car? Like in another three years, she'll have a *six* year old Minicar . . . with 75,000 miles on it . . .

Let's take a look at the two hypothetical cars after three years. Had Mary kept the Maxicruiser, it would now be showing about 132,000 miles. If she had serviced the car properly during those miles, chances are good that she would have had no major problems. The Minicar would now be reading 75,000 miles. It, too, would probably not have needed any major repairs.

The Maxi was worth $1000 three years ago. If it still looks and drives well, it's still worth at least $500. The Mini was worth $6000 three years ago when Mary bought it. At six years and 75,000 miles, it has a market value of about $2000. That's $3500 more depreciation on the Minicar!

OK, let's recap. For the life of the contract, it cost Mary $150 per month more to drive the Minicar than the old one would have, and at the end of those three years, the Maxi had depreciated $500, the Mini, $4000. This is economy?

If Mary could *afford* to shell out all that money over the course of three years, and if she had consciously decided that she would *rather* spend this money on replacing her present car than on a down payment on a house or a lengthy vacation in the tropics, then there was nothing wrong with her purchase.

If, on the other hand, she purchased her Minicar the way a lot of people do--not really aware of the actual costs--she deprived herself of things more important than having a car that blended better in the office parking lot.

One more "if": If Mary had opted for a new car instead of one three years old, her expenses could have been thousands of dollars higher.

In addition to doing your math when deciding what is and what isn't an "economy car," it's also important to decide *whether* to even buy the newer car in the first place. Of course, this presumes that you're really, truly seeking economy!

Figure All the Expenses

The lesson here is to figure in *all* the expenses, not just gas mileage. *The difference in gas mileage from one car to another is almost never a good reason to change cars.* Certainly, if you are about to replace your present car anyway, and fuel economy is a factor, you would be wise to pay attention to the mileage figures of your prospective purchase. But buying a more expensive car simply because of its better mileage requires some careful arithmetic to make an intelligent choice.

Smaller Doesn't Always Mean Cheaper

In today's used-car market, bigger cars are almost always bargains compared to the little "fuel-efficient" models. If you can buy a nice, big, comfortable cruiser for a thousand dollars less than a miniature car in comparable condition, you might *never* save enough on gas to pay the difference. And the bigger cars generally go farther before needing major repairs. Let's use another example. You need a car, and you just happen to be in love with a mid-eighties Eldorado. Your conscience tells you that you should buy a Honda to save money on gas. You drive 15,000 miles per year, mostly highway.

An '86 Eldo with the overdrive transmission will get an easy 20 MPG, highway. Let's give the Honda a break and say it will do 40 MPG. In a 15,000-mile year, the Eldo would use 750 gallons of gas; the Honda 375. At $1.50/gallon, it would cost $563 more per year to drive the Eldo. If you planned to keep either car for three years, and you paid $1500 less for the Eldorado than for the newer Honda, the overall cost of operating the two cars would be the same. Time to shop around.

Not everyone loves big cars. I do, and if I had a certain amount of money available to buy a car, I would always choose an older cruiser over a newer econo-car for the same amount of money.

Matter of fact, that is exactly what I do. My family car has always been a loaded cruiser bought for peanuts because it showed seventy- or eighty-thousand (or more) miles on the odometer. It was always selected because of its as-new condition and the obvious (and often documented) care that it had received. I've never had to do a major repair to any of these cars and I have driven several of them, without a hitch, to well over 150,000 miles. (For an in-depth discussion on high-mile cars, see Chapter 1.)

Summary

If you're really looking for economy, and that means the cheapest miles for your transportation dollars, there's a lot more to consider than gas mileage.

You need to factor in financing costs as opposed to buying a more affordable car for cash, the added insurance required if you do finance the car, and depreciation, the biggest expense in most car-owners' experience.

Almost every one of these considerations points to buying an older car that you can afford to buy for cash.

What counts is *miles per dollar*, not miles per gallon.

SPECIAL INTEREST CARS
or, How to Get Excited About Your Next Car!

Alright, do you ever dream about owning one of those lovely exotics, like a Jaguar or a Mercedes? Can you see yourself in a really beautiful Alfa Romeo convertible or an MG roadster? How about a '65 Mustang, or some other nostalgic jewel? Well, contrary to a popular myth, you *can* have your cake and eat it, too! If you've been reading this book and are more-or-less agreeing that the ideas presented make sense, but that this "objective and sensible" approach to car-buying takes out a lot of the fun, read on.

As you know, a new car is only "new" for a short period of time. Actually, as soon as you sign the papers and drive off, you are driving just another used car. Want proof? Turn around and go back to the dealer. Tell him you just received notice that you're being transferred to Paris and need to get rid of the car at once. You will be informed in no uncertain terms that you are now driving just another used car. And wait till the dealer tells you what it's worth!

A new Toyota, Honda or even a Lexus or a Lincoln is, at best, exactly like thousands of other cars. It is not distinctive or unique, regardless of how much it cost. It is hardly noticeable in a parking lot when brand new, and nearly invisible a few months down the road. (Ever wondered why your car key suddenly didn't work, only to find out you tried to unlock the wrong car?)

Some time ago, I visited an upscale real-estate office with my teenage son. In the parking lot were mostly very expensive, new Japanese luxury cars. My son rattled off some names, like Lexus and Infiniti.

All thirty thousand and up, he told me. (At sixteen, my son was quite the expert on the prices of luxury cars.) Well, right about in the middle of the row of Japan's best was this gorgeous, dark-blue Jaguar sedan, maybe ten years old. Guess which car stood out from the crowd? Guess which one got all the attention? Guess which one was actually worth about *one-third* of what the cheapest of those new Japanese cars cost? Matter of fact, the Jag was worth about the same amount as the *depreciation* one of the other cars suffered when it was driven off the showroom floor!

OK, here's a quick quiz:

1. Are you the type of woman who really enjoys (or would enjoy) owning and driving a distinctive auto?

2. Are you torn between the economic advantages and disadvantages of spending the necessary money to fix your existing car (knowing that its market value will never support the expenditure)?

3. Do you place a certain value on driving a car that doesn't look like every other car?

4. Would you love to figure out a way to turn your transportation budget from a large liability into an attractive investment and in the bargain own an outstanding, eye-catching automobile that will *never* depreciate?

If you answered "yes" to the above questions, then you're definitely a candidate for a special interest car. This isn't for everyone, and if this topic doesn't do anything for you, then you might as well skip the whole chapter. But if there's even a spark of interest (curiosity?), you owe it to yourself to explore the special-interest car concept. And if you're interested, but have the feeling that somehow this is a "guy thing," please read on.

What's a Special Interest Car?

Let me define "special-interest" as it refers to cars. One of my editors told me I should use the word "classic," as everybody knows what a classic car is. Well, therein lies the rub. To a lot of people, any *old* car is a "classic." Even some newspaper classifieds use a heading of "classics" for any car that's more than a few years old. To car enthusiasts, there is a distinct difference between a classic and a special-interest car. A classic is not only a very old car, but one of exceptional quality, style and performance. In some cases, exceptions might be made for perhaps one of those qualifications, but rarely. We're talking vintage Packards, Rolls Royces, and Stutz Bearcats here. Cars, many of which are worth hundreds of thousands of dollars.

If you're going to venture into the arena of specialty cars, it's good to know that these terms have very different meanings to those who live, love and work there. It's all part of being car-savvy.

A "special-interest" car can be both distinctive and unique, and become ever more so as it ages. Special-interest cars cover a wide range. In its most accurate definition, "special-interest" means that a car is of special interest to collectors, which also implies that the car is somewhat rare and therefor pricey. In our discussion, we'll broaden that definition to include all sorts of older-but-classy cars that are still very affordable.

The real special interest cars include such sought-after numbers as the first Pontiac GTOs, the earliest Thunderbirds, "300 series" Chryslers, early

Corvettes, '55 through '57 Chevy Nomads, and such esoterica. From there, *our* definition gets diluted somewhat to include just about any car that's of special interest to *you*. (This is, after all, about you!)

This special interest might be based on nothing more than nostalgia, or it might be based upon a long standing admiration of a certain make and model. Depending on how old you are, it could be a car you've admired ever since high-school!

The advantages of owning a special interest car are several. First of all, in one fell swoop, you will have eliminated one of the most costly aspects of automobile ownership: depreciation. One thing all special interest cars have in common is that (assuming, of course, they are maintained properly and not damaged) *they do not depreciate*. On the contrary; they are investments. Of course, this presumes that you don't pay way too much for the car, and we'll go into this a little later.

Special interest cars are not necessarily *old* cars, either. For example, let's say that ever since Cadillac introduced its Seville in 1976 you have been admiring these beautiful cars. The first Sevilles were of an uncommonly tasteful design, devoid of lots of the superfluous doodads GM liked to tack on their seventies cars. They have become somewhat of a collector's car, but to date have not appreciated much. This makes the car a "sleeper" as far as value is concerned. Very nice, well-maintained examples can be found for under $5000.

An automobile of this stature, particularly one in as-new condition, attracts more than its share of the exact kind of attention that most people expect (and rarely get) when they bring home the brand-new car they just drove off the dealer's showroom floor. Today's new cars (which all seem to resemble huge jelly beans) are so ordinary looking that a lot of folks feel it necessary to leave the price sticker in the window for months after the purchase just to make sure that all of their acquaintances and neighbors realize that this is indeed a new car. Not necessary with a special interest car. (Personally, I think it would be embarrassing to admit to the world that I had just paid $22,000 for a new Honda.)

How about the '65 through '69 Mustangs? Excellent personal cars, always popular, and there are still enough around that they are very affordable. Even a professionally-restored, like-new Mustang of that era can be found for under $10,000. These cars are comfortable, drive well, handle well, they're safe and sturdy, small enough to be easily parked, and yet have more interior space than a lot of new cars of similar outside proportions. They're flashy but not ostentatious, and always attention-getters. Most have power steering and brakes, and a lot of them have air-conditioning. *And they'll never depreciate.*

Another example: ever envied somebody who can afford to own a Jaguar, Mercedes or some other exotic ride like that? When you see some gorgeous, sexy Mercedes convertible cruise by, do you know what year the car is? Couldn't that Mercedes, for all you know, be an exceptional example of a ten-year-old car? Did you know that you can buy an excellent ten-year-old, just-like-new Mercedes for less than the price of many new disposable econo-cars? Hmmmmm, she says!

Many of the world's most prestigious cars are nearly ageless in their designs, meaning that a ten-year-old car looks enough like a two-year-old one that most people don't know the difference.

It's all a matter of personal taste. Some folks are embarrassed to be seen in anything but a "new" car, even if the new car is a bottom-of-the-line cheapo. Others would much prefer a classy, obviously well-maintained older car to *any* new car, not only because of being seen in and associated with such a vehicle, but also because *owning and keeping up an older car is an effective to sidestep nearly every level of the automobile business; one of the most parasitic industries to ever become an essential part of our everyday lives.*

OK, what about repairs?

With a well-chosen special interest car, there is never the question of whether or not it is financially prudent to make a necessary repair. Example: you own a six-year-old econo-import in fairly nice shape. The car has ninety- thousand miles on it and the transmission is acting up. The repair shop informed you that it's just a matter of time before you will be facing a five-hundred dollar repair bill. It is now decision time.

The car has already depreciated to under $2000, assuming no transmission problems. (Don't dwell on the fact that you paid over $8000 for it . . .) Should you just sell it the way it is and take you lumps now, or spend yet another $500 that you'll never recover? If you opt to spend the money to fix the car, you'll feel obliged to keep it for another few years "to get your money back out." But what if it needs another major repair in the near future? It's always a dead-end street.

If the car in question happened to be a 1969 Mustang, a 1982 Mercedes or Jaguar, a 1972 Cutlass convertible, or any other excellent example of the car of your dreams, there is no question about repairs or the money spent on them. Money spent on maintaining a special interest car is, almost without exception, like putting money in the bank.

I've had several women tell me, yes, they'd had fantasies about having an older Mercedes SL convertible, or maybe a '66 Mustang, but that it was a "guy thing." They believed that since these cars were old, they would also be undependable and in need of constant attention. Not so!

Think about this for a moment: why would a carefully-restored ten-, twenty- or even thirty-year-old car be any less dependable than it was when new? The fact is, these older cars (especially the American ones) have a level of simplicity that makes them as dependable as *any* new car today, and in many cases, more so. Plus, if anything ever *does* go wrong, they're easily fixed by anyone with basic repair-knowledge. (And that *could* be you!)

Sounds Good So Far?

If this notion gets you a little excited, start looking over the "collector's cars" section in the classified section of any major newspaper. Or pick up a copy of Hemmings Motor News, check prices on cars you like, and get a feel for what the values are. Hemmings is available on many news stands, or you can call 1-800-227-4373 for a sample copy and subscription info. (You can also find their Web Page on the 'Net by typing Hemming's into your search utility. On their Web Page, you can request a free sample issue.)

Of course, a classified will do little to inform you of the *real* condition of a car, but the overall picture will begin to emerge after researching it for a while. (It's been my experience that advertisers in Hemmings Motor News are generally more objective and less optimistic in describing their cars than those who advertise in newspaper classifieds. Perhaps this is partly because Hemmings is read worldwide, and mainly by auto enthusiasts.)

Think about some of the cars you've admired for years. Wouldn't you like to finally own one? Look through the ads and see what they're going for. Check your pulse as you read through the ads! Special interest and/or collector's cars are becoming big business. A few years ago, it was only the *truly* special interest cars that were appreciating. Now it's just about any car that's old, or even newer ones that are in some unique way interesting. But it's definitely not too late to get in on the ground floor of this fulfilling adventure in auto ownership.

If you start looking for a particular make, model and year of car, look at lots of ads to get a feel for asking prices. They can vary a lot depending on the seller's personal reasons, and one or two prices don't establish a value. <u>Hemmings</u> has the most realistic prices, and the tabloid-size "auto-trader" type of local publications usually have the highest. And don't forget: an asking price rarely ends up being the selling price!

A little side note: I just looked in the current issue of <u>Hemmings</u> and counted 353 *ads* just for 1964-1970 Mustangs. Most of these cars are either fully restored or in excellent original condition. There are more exciting deals on special-interest cars out there than you can imagine!

Buy a Restored Car

Unless you're already experienced in the restoration of old cars (!) or have an unlimited budget, it is almost always a better idea to buy a car that is either in excellent original condition or which someone has had professionally refurbished, than to buy one in need of complete restoration and then have to deal with finding the talent to restore it. The original car in excellent original condition is a good way to go, but these are getting harder to find.

Nice originals are much easier to find in the kinds of cars that have not yet made it to highly-sought-after status. The chapters on checking out the mechanical and body condition of any used car apply to these cars as well, but it is not at all unusual to find the owner of a special interest car having complete records of all service and repairs ever done to the car. The ever-increasing prices of new cars makes the decent older ones worth more, so even a plain-vanilla sedan that's ten years old but in pristine condition is now often worth more than it cost new. Of course, that was back when a dollar was still worth fifty cents.

Step Into an Investment Auto!

Remember way back in the seventies when you could buy a brand new Toyota Corolla or a Mercury Capri for $2400? Or how about a new '65 Mustang for $2495?! Back in the seventies, there were rumors afloat in the auto industry that it was about to take the American public on the most outrageous one-way roller-coaster ride they had ever seen. There were predictions from Madison Avenue of cars costing over $20,000 by 1990, and those predictions (read: promises) were accompanied by statements that the whole program would be so well-pulled-off that our well-conditioned consumers would fully accept those kinds of prices by then. Well, guess what?

You *can* step off of that roller-coaster, you know. A special interest car is just one way to do it, but if you have ever had the inclination, there has never been a better time.

If you have the desire to drive a prestigious automobile, here are some things to consider: if you drop over twenty grand (forty isn't uncommon these days) on a new cruiser, in a few years it will be nothing but another plain old used car, upstaged by all the new flash from the automaker's latest efforts and worth about half (or less) what you paid for it. Spending ten thousand dollars on a beautiful, pampered, ten-year-old prestige ride like a top-of-the-line Mercedes may make better economic sense. Then put the other ten grand in the bank to collect interest, buy a houseful of new furniture, or a vacation in Rio. Your impeccable and impressive special-interest car will continue to impress . . . and be a pleasure to own and operate for many years, while the new $20,000+ car will decline in all areas; value, appearance and function. Most new cars depreciate about 30% of their new-price when you sign on as the first owner. That's the exact moment a new car becomes a used car. And as soon as you get it out on the road, it will disappear in a sea of millions of other used cars just like it.

Trivia: in upscale automotive circles, cars are always referred to as *automobiles* when they are prestigious. If they are uncommonly prestigious, they are called *motorcars*!

But what about all my favorite options?

A look through some "collector's cars" classifieds will undoubtedly bring back some pleasant memories of cars you really liked in years gone by. Even if you demand all the comforts and accessories offered in newer cars, remember that almost all of them were available in the expensive cars of ten, twenty and even thirty years ago. Even some fifties cars had air-conditioning and power-assisted steering, brakes, seats, and windows. Almost all high-end domestic cars of the sixties had all of these features available. And how long has it been since you've driven an older car? After getting used to smaller cars over the years, you might not like a big car any more at all. But then, you just might. Give it a try.

The 60's and 70's cars

Sixties and seventies domestic doesn't have to mean big, either. One example of a small, desirable sixties car is the Buick Skylark. These cars looked a little like reduced-size versions of the full-size Buick, except that the designers did such a fine job that the cars didn't have that "shrunken/miniature" look that many similar efforts have produced. These cars were available in '61 through '63, in sedans, convertibles, hardtop coupes and wagons. The '61 and '62 are the most sought-after, but are still available in nice condition for around $5000. Compared to what they cost new, that may seem a bit much. But compared to what you can buy in a late-model ordinary-just-like-everyone-else's car for the same money, it's a bargain. Especially when you consider that a $5000 generic used car will be worth $500 in a few years and the Skylark will just keep appreciating forever.

Other small-car options include the foreign sports cars, like the MG, Fiat convertible, and such. Some of the era's sports cars were available in sedans, too, if you don't like ragtops. MG had a wonderful model, the MGB-GT, and there were all sorts of interesting small imported sedans in that era, too.

Those Mustangs again

Mustangs, from the first ones up through 1970, are excellent small-car investments. Like the ads in Hemmings illustrate, there are lots of beautifully-restored, just like new Mustangs on the market, and many are in the $10,000 range. And a lot less, if you make a lucky find. What kind of new car will that money buy, and what will it be worth next year?

If you're concerned with parts availability on older cars, fret not! For any of the popular ones, like the Mustangs, there are more parts available for them now then there were when they were nearly new! There are numerous after-market manufacturers making every piece for these wonderful cars. Everything is available new: body and mechanical parts, and even complete interior upholstery kits. And these cars are so simple to work on that any competent mechanic can service them, unlike new cars with all their electronic control-systems.

Exotics and (Real) Sports Cars

If your desires run to something a little more exotic, like perhaps an XJS Jaguar or even a Triumph TR6 or MGB, have the car gone over *very carefully*, and by someone familiar with the particular make and model. Make absolutely certain that you are not looking at a rebuilt wreck. (Chapters 14 & 15 tell you how to do that.) Remember, you're buying this car as an investment. These cars, like Jaguars, Porshes, and Alfas, *can* be expensive to maintain. But even so, purchased for a fair price, they are still a good investment. And there is also a lot of myth to the reputation of unreliability, too. A lot of these cars were bought new by people who drove them hard and didn't maintain them well. They didn't like that. I've known Jaguars, even the really old ones with the worst reputations, that made it to well over 100,000 miles before needing any significant repairs, but they were driven carefully and well-maintained. MG's and Triumphs were excellent cars; dependable, good performers, and they get great gas mileage. Mechanically, they are definitely not in the exotic category, and are easily maintained and repaired by any competent mechanic. And talk about a fun ride!

Many makes of older cars enjoy such popularity that owner's organizations have been formed to support keeping these cars on the road forever. Membership in these clubs is highly recommended, if for no other purpose than the fine parts and information resources that they are. Most of them have Internet listings, with owner/enthusiast discussion groups. If you're into 'Net surfing, type your pet make of car into a search utility and see what comes up. You'll be surprised at how much is out there. You can even enter into one of the discussion groups and ask for any info that you'd like regarding the car of your dreams. The Internet is also an excellent resource for finding specific cars and parts.

What about gas mileage on these older cars? Well, a lot of the imports and sports cars will get 25 mpg and better. The domestic cars don't do as well. Some get pretty decent mileage, like in the low twenties, but even that doesn't compare well to the 30 mpg you can expect from most new cars. But consider this: your *total* gas expenses over the first few years of ownership will be less than just the *depreciation* you'll suffer on a new car. Any new car. For a detailed discussion on this topic, please read Chapter 4, Miles per Gallon vs. Miles per Dollar.

Chapters 14 through 16 will guide you through the process of checking out a prospective purchase. The techniques are the same as for a newer car. However, since the possibility of reconditioning becomes greater as a car ages, I strongly recommend that you seek the counsel of professionals in making a final evaluation, particularly if this is an expensive purchase and/or one which you want to keep for years. Any good body shop can look over a car and tell you what body repairs have been done. Be sure to have them look underneath, too!

Engine Swapping

My *original* opening paragraph for this chapter suggested that since this is going to be some techno-speak, you might want to skip it for now, or maybe remember where it is in case you ever need it; it'll be a lot more interesting then. This is where one of my editors went ballistic! Her comment: "I strongly disagree with you guiding women to skip this so-called techno-speak. This is good info, and they should be encouraged to read it and know it."

Well, here it is. An obvious question asked by folks just becoming interested in the possibilities offered by special-interest car ownership is, "What happens if I ever need something major, like an engine, for an out-of-production car?"

Let's say you own this absolutely wonderful 1954 Studebaker Commander Starlight Coupe, and it needs an engine. Now what? Not many dismantlers are likely to have in stock a fresh, low-mileage Studebaker engine, but you still have at least two alternatives. One is, of course, an overhauled engine. The other is a nice, fresh, low-mileage engine from an entirely different make of car. (The very thought of an engine-swap on any collector car is enough to make many enthusiasts violently ill, if not violent . . . but please read on.)

Adaptors are available which can bolt together some of the most unlikely combinations of engines and transmissions. Many auto-parts stores have a catalog of these and can order one for you. There are whole adaptor kits available for some of these swaps. They include the engine-to-transmission adaptor and the engine-mounts and any other hardware needed to make the swap.

Admittedly, engine swapping is something which must be done by a competent mechanic. I suggest that you never engage the services of a mechanic who has not successfully done other swaps or who expresses disdain when approached with the possibility. Clearly, this kind of work is best done by someone who enjoys doing it.

There's no magic involved. Anyone who is mechanically competent, has the facilities to do the job, and enjoys working on cars, can do engine swaps. I stress the part about enjoying the work and feel it's important in this kind of project, mostly because it requires patience, something a lot of mechanics are short on. It's time-consuming simply because of the little nit-picking details like adapting and rerouting fuel lines, throttle linkage and such. The end result, however, can be very rewarding and worth all the soon-forgotten frustrations.

There's an important side-benefit to *you, the owner*, being around during the work, be it an engine-swap or just maintenance: you become more familiar with your automobile. This familiarity can produce a feeling for the car which lets you know immediately if something is not right, and a competence in determining what it is.

Another, and often preferred, solution to engine-swapping is to use an engine/transmission package and forget about adaptors. This way, you will need to adapt transmission mounts as well as engine mounts, but you will have dispensed with any intangibles of mating an engine to a different transmission. I've seen quite a few of these installations where the only change necessary to mount the new transmission was to drill new holes in the transmission-mounting crossmember.

Remember that engine-swapping in some special-interest cars *can* seriously reduce their value. If yours is simply an older car whose main value is its excellent condition, this wouldn't apply. But installing the "wrong" engine in a genuine collector car would be a wise choice only if you planned to keep the car forever, didn't care about the car's value, and/or if you were immune to the disparaging remarks from collector-car buffs. (I endured these remarks for years while driving a remarkable Jaguar in which I installed a Chevrolet engine and transmission. Installing the Chevy components dramatically improved the performance, gas mileage and handling of the Jaguar. It also turned it into a very dependable machine, something Jaguars, particularly ones that have seen less than adequate maintenance, are rarely accused of being.)

And don't forget <u>Hemmings Motor News</u> as an excellent resource for parts . . . anything from frames to door handles. The publication lists each make in its own section, and divides that section into subsections for parts and cars. Chapter 17 covers dealing with auto-dismantlers and their hot-line access to parts all over the country.

Overhauls

Assuming that an engine swap is out of the question, let's discuss the other alternative, that "O" word, the overhauled engine. (See Chapter 17 for an in-depth discussion of overhauls.) Since I have not yet seen an acceptable overhauled engine, I'm not in a position to offer any referrals. But in an effort to be of some assistance, I've interviewed some collector-car people. They were all of the same opinion: it is extremely difficult to find a shop capable of satisfactory overhauls. Most of them did, however, have a favorite; a shop which was the only place they would go for an overhaul.

Incidently, the terms "overhauled" and "rebuilt" are used interchangeably. Some shops will tell you that one means a more though job than the other. Getting a list of exactly what will be done is the only way to tell what you're getting.

My suggestion is to use this same resource when you decide you need an engine rebuilt: find a collector and ask for a referral. Better yet, find several. How do you find a serious collector? A lot of auto-parts stores can direct you to customers who are old-car enthusiasts. You can always talk to the owner of a nice, older car you happen across in a parking lot. Most of these folks are happy to help out another car buff. Special-interest or vintage auto shows are one of the easiest ways to get lots of feedback. And there's always the Internet. If you're a 'Net Surfer, give it a try. Type your favorite car into a search utility and you'll be amazed at what comes up.

But make sure that you get engine-overhaul referrals from collector-car enthusiasts, not hot-rod or racing people. There are distinct differences between the disciplines involved in building engines whose main focus is maximum power and those whose quiet dependability is essential. Always go to the person who is the specialist in the field you are interested in.

When you find your prospective overhaul shop, talk to the owner/manager and ask to see the machine shop. You can usually tell a lot about the care which goes into a person's product by observing the condition of his workspace. Also ask for an explanation of the processes your engine will go through in its overhaul, and discuss the results with your car-savvy friend. Before signing the work order, get in writing a list of the new parts that will go into your overhaul.

Summary

Ownership of a special-interest car can be an extremely rewarding experience in many ways. There's nothing special or difficult about the maintenance of these cars. Matter of fact, when you find yourself owning a car with a real personality, you might be inspired to do your own basic maintenance (or at least watch when somebody else does it), and become friends with your car in the process. Tune-ups and basic repairs are also a lot cheaper on older cars than on the computer-controlled newer models, and with few exceptions, parts availability is excellent.

Owners of these cars are generally totally immune to the rantings of the auto-advertising world. They are immune to planned obsolescence and depreciation. They don't have to tolerate the high-tech nonsense of all new cars; all the computer gadgetry that makes it impossible to maintain their own cars. They don't have to endure the cheap, flimsy construction and shoddy assembly evident in so many new cars, particularly domestic models. This group of car owners will have the most noteworthy autos on the block; this year, next year and on down the line, and you often see them driving around wearing big grins.

THE TRADE-IN

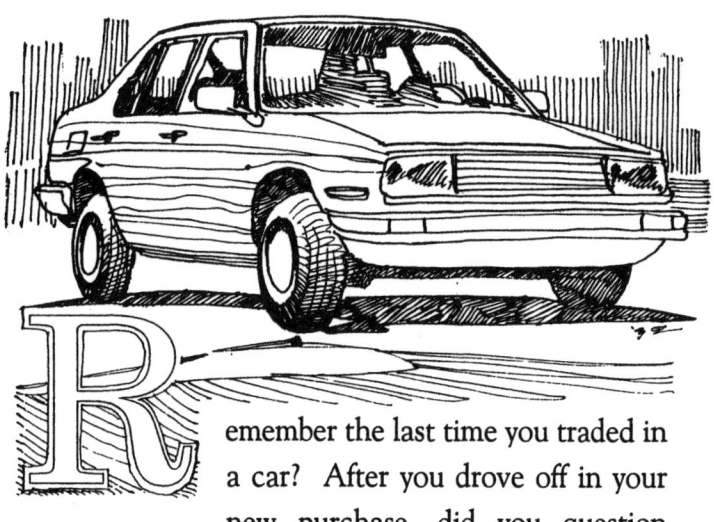

Remember the last time you traded in a car? After you drove off in your new purchase, did you question whether or not you really got a fair deal? Understanding the trade-in game needn't be difficult, although it often seems so. This is a short chapter because it only needs to make one simple point.

Recently, a bright young woman called me and said that a friend to whom I had sold several cars

Recently, a bright young woman called me and said that a friend to whom I had sold several cars recommended that she ask me to find her the specific car she was looking for.

She said her budget was about $6000. Definitely a used-car budget. But then she said she was also considering a new car, *because the new-car dealers offered her more for her trade-in.*

OK, let's talk about the sales-pitch, "... more for your trade-in."

Her present car had an actual cash value (ACV) of about $1000. That's what the car would bring at wholesale auction, give or take $100. *To any dealer, what the car will bring at auction is the actual cash value.* The ACV is what the dealer will allow, in real dollars, on your trade-in. Period. Never more, and usually less.

Listen very carefully: If a dealer offers $1500 for a trade-in with a $1000 ACV, *he is simply adding the $500 difference to the price of the car he's selling.*

New cars, particularly those with a lot of optional extras, have far more profit-margin spread for the dealer to work with than do most used cars. The greater the spread, the greater the opportunity to "offer more" on the trade-in.

Fact: no dealer is going to give you more than Actual Cash Value for your trade-in. But almost nobody believes this! Over and over, I hear the same old story. . . . "I bought it from Whatsizface Motors because he gave me $1000 more for my old junk than anyone else would."

HE DID NOT!!! HE GAVE YOU ACV AND CHARGED YOU $1000 MORE FOR YOUR NEW CAR THAN HE WOULD HAVE IF YOU HAD NOT TRADED IN YOUR OLD CAR!!!

This isn't exclusive to new car dealers, either. You can go to a half-dozen used car lots and get way different quotes on what they'll allow you on your old car. Some of it has to do with how much the dealer has invested in the particular car he's trying to sell you. The only thing you need to know is that the arithmetic never changes: You're going to get ACV for your car, no matter how they make the numbers look on paper.

An Example

Try this: you're selling your old clunker. You figure you need about $1000 for it, but you haven't told anybody. Your neighbor, Sarah, says she'll buy it from you if you take her riding mower in on trade. She never uses it, and you mentioned to her some time ago that you'd be interested in buying it. You think it's worth $300.

Sarah tells you that she needs to get $600 for her mower. So you tell her that you'll sell her your car for $1300 and give her the $600 trade-in for her mower. Everybody's happy, right? Sarah can now feel that she "sold" you her mower for $600, even though you allowed her only $300 by raising the price of your car by $300. Isn't this fun?

This is exactly how it works with a lot of car buyers. How much they're going to get for that trade-in is more important to them than the price of the car they're buying, and that suits the dealer just fine.

Sell Your Old Car Yourself!

Go to three or four dealers and ask them what they will pay you for your car. Cash sale. You're moving to Iceland and are *not* in the market for a car. You need to get rid of the one you have, and what would they give you for it? You can safely figure that the highest offer you get for the car on a CASH SALE is pretty close to its ACV.

Once you know the actual cash value of your car, do the sensible thing and sell it yourself. Run an ad in the paper. If you're in a hurry to sell it, price it at at about half-way between what the dealers offered and what the same year and model cars are advertised for in the classifieds (which will always be higher).

Sure, sometimes it can be a hassle selling your own car, and you feel you just have to trade it in. But before you run down to Auto Row, consider this. What if you ran an ad, talked to a half dozen prospective buyers, and finally sold the car for three or four hundred dollars more than the dealers offered you for it? How long did it take you to do all that? A couple of hours?

Even if it took three or four hours, $100 an hour is pretty good compensation, isn't it?

You are always in a better position to deal if you do not have a trade-in. You are at a distinct disadvantage if you *need* to trade in your old car in order to buy the new one.

Summary:

The trade-in is one of the most powerful tools in the dealer's customer-manipulation bag. If you have a trade, the dealer has the upper hand as soon as you drive onto the lot, and he'll likely keep it. If you're not convinced and you're *still* going to trade it in, remember, *no dealer is going to give you more than ACV for that car.* If he says he will, he's just adding the difference onto the price of the car he's selling. That's the truth, the whole truth and nothing but the truth.

DEALER AUCTIONS

verything You Ever Wanted to Know About Auctions But Didn't Care Enough to Ask . . . or, why *should* I care? That was the alternate title for this chapter!

It's really simple. The more you expand your how-the-car-selling-business-works consciousness, the less likely you'll be a target for a con-job. Con-jobs are pervasive throughout the car business, right down to the trip your neighbor might try to lay on you about the car s/he's trying to sell you. It's amazing how selling a car can make a dishonest person out of just about anybody! But the dealers and their sales-people are pros at this game and much evidence supports the notion that women are favored targets. The more you know about how the game works, the better your position. It's difficult to fool somebody who is well-informed!

Although you'll probably never attend a wholesale auto auction, it's to your advantage to know what goes on there and how it fits into the whole picture of retail auto sales.

The wholesale dealers' auction allows licensed auto dealers to buy and sell cars in an environment that excludes the retail public. The auction is not necessarily a place to unload lemons.

Why do dealers take perfectly good cars to the auctions? In the normal course of business, retail auto dealers end up owning vehicles which, for various reasons, they choose not to offer for sale on their lots. Most of these vehicles are their trade-ins.

Here's what might happen: one dealer just hates Ford Escorts. Maybe he had one come apart on him once and he spent a bundle on it trying to get it made right. So, now he'll take one in on trade if he can steal it, but because of his attitude about Escorts (whether justified or not), this car *will* go to the auction. He just doesn't want it on his lot.

Other dealers specialize in certain types of cars, and any other trade-ins just don't fit in. Those also go to the auction.

Lease companies use auctions to liquidate their cars when they reach a certain mileage; some of the best late-model cars I've ever bought were ex-lease vehicles. Banks and finance companies also use auctions to get rid of their repossessions, which in tough times, come through by the hundreds.

Rebuilt Wrecks

A high percentage of the cars offered for sale at auctions are not what they appear to be. Although some truly fine cars do come through, wholesale dealers' auctions are the outlet of choice for rebuilders and lemon dealers.

Some of the cars that show up at auctions every week are so obviously trashed-together wrecks, that it's hard to believe anyone would buy them, especially a professional dealer. But there are enough shaky dealers willing to resell anything they can buy cheap, to keep these sellers in business.

Where do these dubious autos come from? Well, what do you suppose happens to cars that get wrecked, the ones the insurance companies pay off as "totals?" They go to "salvage pools" and are auctioned off to the highest bidder.

From there, most of the cars which, by any stretch of the imagination, can be rebuilt are bought by rebuilders and will appear on the market again, most likely at the wholesale auctions.

In an effort to insure that these cars will *not* be rebuilt and sold without disclosing to the buyer that the car has been damaged, some states have rulings making it mandatory for insurance companies to turn in the title of any car they pay off in full, in other words, a "total."

Unfortunately, there are lots of holes in these rulings. The biggest one is that it is still quite easy to ship wrecked cars to another state, one that has no such rules. This is common practice. Many truckloads of these insurance totals are shipped to states which allow re-registering the cars with a minimum of hassle.

The "accident business," from the moment the damaged car is towed from the scene to whatever its ultimate destiny might be, offers almost limitless opportunities to unscrupulous individuals. And unfortunately, nobody seems to care because it doesn't seem to matter what an insurance company's costs are. They adjust our premiums to make up the difference and to maintain their enormous profits.

All of the dealer auctions declare that they won't tolerate rebuilds. But even if the auction management makes a genuine effort to exclude rebuilt cars (and most of them now do), it is next to impossible to screen out all of them.

The wholesale dealers' auction is the outlet for all of these cars: everything from exceptional to unacceptable. And with such a variety, a dealer has to keep on his toes at every moment if he's going to stay in business long. Many retail dealers rely almost exclusively on auctions to keep their inventory supplied.

There are Good Cars at the Auctions!

There are decent vehicles at auto auctions. There are also decent dealers who will pay the top-dollar prices these cars easily bring. It's important to know this, because "cars from auctions" often receive a lot of unwarranted negative press. I'll show you how to find the decent dealers and how to identify the exceptional cars.

Here is one example of how truly excellent cars find their way to dealer auctions. Someone has just traded in his six-year-old, loaded Olds Regency Brougham with 19,000 miles on it on a one-year-old Honda Civic, in order to "get better gas mileage." A six-year-old, top-of-the-line Olds with 19K on the clock (as they say) is premium merchandise.

The Honda dealer could put it on his lot at $1000 over retail "book" and see what happens. (Chapter 8 explains "the book.") It might sell right away, but the chances are it wouldn't. Most buyers would much rather have his other Regency Brougham, the one showing 55,000 miles, for $1000 less money.

But at the auction, there will be hundreds of dealers from all over the home and neighboring states. With all those dealers, the chances are better than excellent that one of them has a customer waiting for just this car. That dealer, who has a sure sale awaiting him, will pay the price.

Often, when a dealer comes across an exceptional vehicle with low miles, and which shows all the signs of having had loving care, he doesn't even try to retail it; it goes right to the auction. Why?

One reason might be that he knows from experience that most of *his* buying public doesn't know the difference between a truly fine car and a well-detailed, just-average one. In that case, he's wasting his time trying to sell the exceptional car on his own lot, when he can sell the "look-alike" (another same make, model and year, but with higher miles) a lot cheaper. As in the examples above, there can be an amazing difference in the values of two cars which may look identical to the uninformed buyer. A dealer who has both a sharp eye and a clientele who knows the difference, is willing to pay that difference. The customer who thinks he can buy the "same" car down the road for a whole lot less lacks this vision.

Lease Returns

Some of the best buys at dealer auctions are lease returns. These are usually current-year or one-year-old cars, and are generally in top condition.

They'll usually have from ten to twenty-five thousand miles on them and will be available with a wide range of options. Lease returns often make up the bulk of the inventory on a large new-car store's used-car lot.

Dealers eagerly buy up these cars because, of the cars that they take in trade, only a small percentage are good enough to retail on their lots. If they had to rely on trades to keep their lots full, they'd be in trouble because most people don't trade in their old ride until it's beginning to wear out or it has some major flaw which they think can be hidden from the dealer.

A lot of dealers will readily deny that they get some of their cars at auctions because of that negative opinion much of the public seems to have about cars bought at auctions.

Just yesterday, I read in a Consumer Reports magazine that " . . . cars coming from wholesale auctions may be of lower quality." I have no idea why they chose to publish this concept, because they could just as well have said that cars coming from wholesale auctions may be of *higher* quality! Both are true.

But now you know better! Once you get to know a dealer you feel you can trust, you can even ask him to watch the auctions for a particular car for you. This works well with lease or rental returns.

Some dealers won't even talk to you about doing this but others will. Some will ask you for a deposit just to confirm that you're serious about buying this car. If you give a deposit, make sure the receipt says that it's 100% refundable if you find the car to be unacceptable for any (reasonable) reason.

It's important to specify exactly what you want, right down to the options and colors, but, of course, the less specific you are, the more likely you will be to get your car. Give preferences, if possible. Like what color you would like best, your second (and third?) choice. If you really aren't particular about color, make sure you specify any color that turns you off! If you tell him you don't care, and he brings you a bright orange car and you say, "No way!," You've lost your deposit!

If there are no lease returns available at the moment and you're in no particular hurry, ask him to call you the next time there's a lease-return sale. He gets announcements from the auctions and will be able to tell you what will be available, too.

Your dealer may not be buying any lease returns for himself at the time you inquire, but if asked for a particular car, he'll be glad to buy one for a customer with cash-in-hand. And since you know that there is an abundance of these cars available, you can even ask him to get you the car for a fixed amount over his cost. I know of several dealers who are happy to do this for one or two hundred dollars.

Summary
As with any business, the more you know about how it works, the better your chances of operating effectively within it. Remember, an informed customer is hard to fool!

As opposed to popular belief, not all cars that come from auctions are substandard. Although there is some truth in the notion that auctions are outlets of choice for a lot of unscrupulous dealers unloading their junk, there are also many really fine autos sold at these auctions.

Most dealers get most of their used-car inventory from the wholesale dealer's auctions. The best cars I've ever bought came from auctions.

Lease-returns are almost always well-maintained cars with low mileage. A large percentage of all lease and rental returns are sold through the dealer's auctions. They are usually detailed and look like new before they go to the auctions. They're almost all well-equipped and can be bought at terrific savings compared to a new car.

If you feel you know and trust a particular independent dealer (preferably a small one), you can ask him to find you any specific car at the auctions.

THE BOOK AND ITS MYSTERY UNRAVELED

AK, you've heard of the "blue book," right? Is it really some kind of last-word authority on what a car is really worth? Maybe you remember hearing something like, "Oh yes, and today only, we can allow you the 'Blue-Book value' on your trade-in."

Or perhaps you've heard this one, "Today only, I can let you have this car for only $100 over wholesale book. Now, that's a deal!"

Just what is this "bible" of the used car business? And why should you even care what this infamous book is all about?

What the book is all about is explained below. What's important is that in car-dealing, a lot of money decisions are based on this book. Dealers and salesmen often use the book's figures to "prove" to their customers the value of both cars they have for sale and those offered in trade. If you need any convincing that your money decisions should *never* be based on these figures, you might want to read this chapter!

There are several versions of "the book." Among them are the <u>Kelley Blue Book</u> and the <u>National Automobile Dealers Association Official Used Car Guide</u>. They're all referred to as "the book."

Each is a regional periodical and there are are several editions of each book. According to the publishers, the several editions contain information specific to various regions of the country; the information the books contain is obtained from auction reports and dealers' retail sales reports, and is as accurate as possible. In this case, "accurate" is a subjective term, making the book an interesting phenomenon.

OK, we're going to launch into a discussion, complete with examples, on why you need to seriously question any numbers from these publications. As you read on, feel free to quit when you feel convinced. The rest of the chapter will be redundant. But until you *are* convinced, please keep reading; it's that important!

Many people, including some dealers, bankers, loan officers and customers make big mistakes and lose a lot of money by assuming that the book provides an accurate reflection of a car's worth. To get any useful information out of the book, it needs to be interpreted by someone who is intimately familiar with current market conditions.

The only way you can learn to interpret the book is by careful, continuous and consistent monitoring of the actual market. Dealers do this by attending auctions, and by reading the market reports published by those auctions. The reports list the year, make, model, odometer-miles and optional equipment of each car; sometimes they also include a code for the condition of the car. All of this information needs to be understood and interpreted to be of any value.

For example, I've sold cars at auction for nearly twice as much money as seemingly identical cars going through the same sale. If they appeared to be identical, why did I get so much more for mine? The reasons are sometimes obvious and sometimes not, especially to the untrained eye.

To a dealer who looks at thousands of cars a year, the difference between a fresh, well-maintained car and a dog which was carefully cleaned up to look like a fresh, well-maintained car, is usually easily detected.

An Example

But here's an example of some of the contradictions that add to the confusion of trying to interpret auction sales-reports. One time I took two identical cars to the auction. They were both same-year Subaru four-wheel-drive wagons, both loaded with all the options, both white with blue interiors. Serious twins. Their appearances suggested that they were both in near-perfect condition. But one car had over eighty-thousand miles on the odometer and the other had forty-thousand.

The high-miler had been meticulously maintained and serviced all its life and the miles were obviously mostly highway. It ran and drove as new. The low mileage car evidently never saw any service at all. The engine was noisy, as was just about everything else mechanical in the car; it didn't drive well at all. But it was professionally detailed to look as good as possible.

The low-mileage car brought two-thousand dollars more than the much better, well-maintained, high-mileage one!

So if the real condition of the car is "easily detected," why did the better car sell for less? Because dealers know that the public has been conditioned to think that the number of miles on the odometer is the most important consideration in judging a car, so cars *showing* low miles are premium units. Actual condition, especially involving flaws which don't show, is secondary to *dealers who have no qualms about selling lemons*; and low-mileage lemons sell quickly.

And here's the point: when the next auction report was printed, it showed the sales of these two cars. What useful information could you get by looking at only these figures? Yet these are the figures the various versions of "the Book" depend on.

More Examples

Here are some more examples of how the book deviates from reality. At any wholesale auction, there are a lot of late-model popular cars that will bring at least $500 more than the book lists as wholesale. A really sharp one can bring up to $1000 over. And that's at the wholesale dealer's level.

Then there are other cars, plain-vanilla sedans and just some specific makes and models that never hit popular status, that will bring somewhere between *half* of their book-value to $500 under.

Some cars in a fully-equipped, four-door version will bring their book value if they're in excellent condition, while the same make, model and year in a two-door will bring about $1500 less than the book says it's worth. A convertible isn't worth much in Minnesota but it's a premium item in Florida or Southern California. Confusing? You bet.

Book Tricks

A trick often used to manipulate book figures to a salesman's advantage is to show the high-mileage deduction-table when appraising a trade-in or to conceal the high-mile deduction when using the book to demonstrate the value of the high-mile car he's trying to sell. Or conversely, showing you the low-mileage add-on table for the car he's trying to sell, but NOT showing it when appraising an incoming car.

Examples: the book directs you to deduct a whopping $1700 from the value of a certain two-year-old mid-sized car showing 80,000 miles on the odometer. Conversely, if your five-year-old similar car has only 35,000 on it, you can add $1000 to its book value. In real life, a sharp five-year-old car with only 35,000 miles on it would likely bring more than just $1000 over its book (depending, of course, on what kind of car it is).

As a basic rule of thumb, the book values presume 15,000 miles per year to be "normal," with anything under or over that amount showing a deduct or an add-on in value. Another common misuse of the book is for a dealer to "prove" the value of one of his cars by showing it to you in an outdated book. For example, if the current book showed the value of a certain car at $8500 today, a three-month-old book might show it as $10,500. You have to look carefully to check the date of issue on each book. It's usually on the cover.

Even bank loan-officers, who use the book in their daily decision-making, get led astray, sometimes in both directions: they might loan more on some cars than they are actually worth on the market, putting both the bank and its customers in a precarious position by granting auto loans on cars that depreciate faster than the loan gets paid down. And they might deny other customers loans when the book fails to reflect the real value of one of the many cars which consistently sell for more than "book" price.

The bottom line is, unless you have the time to research the market, go to every auction you can get into (which is next to impossible without a dealer's license), study every auction report you can find and pay close attention to the changing market trends, *don't rely on the "book" for any information you intend to use in making decisions that can cost you money!*

Summary

The "book" is nearly meaningless to the occasional auto-purchaser. It can even be misleading and dangerous to rely on.

And yes, that was a lot of talk about the notorious "book." But I've seen so many people get burned by accepting the numbers in those books, that I feel I need to present a strong argument to convince you to not rely on them.

There are much more accurate ways to determine the real value of a car. One is to look at the classifieds, find several of the same year, make and model, and average the asking prices. One price won't tell you much because it might be an exceptional car or it might be a real clunker; three or four prices in the same range are a good indication. Bear in mind also that cars can almost always be bought for quite a lot less than the asking prices in the paper.

Another way is to call a dealer on the phone and tell him you need to sell your (fictitious) car. Describe the condition as like-new, give him a low mileage figure and ask for a ballpark price that he would pay outright for the car. Make it clear that you don't want to trade it in.

In a pinch, if there's just no other convenient way for you to accurately determine the value of a car that you're considering buying, you *can* use the book figures, but only under these conditions: You're looking at an average late-model car, in average condition, with average miles (15,000 per year) and you use the "wholesale" amount in the *current book* as the value as a very general figure. (And then go verify it by looking in the classifieds!)

(A little disclaimer here: The above mentions of dealers who have no qualms about selling lemons is not meant to imply that all dealers are like that. A lot of them definitely *are*, but I've also known a number of dealers who do their very best to make sure that the lemons never come onto their lots. They're the kinds of folks you'll want to buy your next car from.)

THE "FTC" STICKER

A few years ago, the Federal Trade Commission, in what they wanted the consumer to believe was an attempt to regulate certain aspects of the auto industry, invented a document known to the public as the "Buyers Guide" and to the trade as the "FTC Sticker." It became law that this document be displayed in a conspicuous manner in all vehicles for sale to the public by dealers. Any violations are punishable by an immediate $10,000 fine per incident.

So now, when you visit any dealer's lot, you will find a prominently-displayed document in the window of each and every used vehicle. That document will inform you about either of two things: that the car has *no warranty* and is being sold as-is, or that the car *has a warranty* and the terms follow, in finer print, on the document itself.

Consumer protection, right? Sure. Turns out that this well-meaning document does little for the customer and does wonders to protect the dealer from customer complaints, no matter how bad the car turns out to be. "FTC" becomes something like "Fool The Customer." Once you've signed the FTC sticker, you have accepted the dealer's terms of sale.

Warranties

Most dealers now act as agents for insurance companies selling "warranties." (See Chapter 11: Insurance.) Often it's a warranty which the dealer advertises as "Two Year Parts and Labor Warranty . . . Covers Every Part of the Car . . . Covers Emergency Road Service . . . Rental Car . . . " and then in fine print, "available." This means that for a price, the dealer will sell you an insurance policy which protects you in the event that the car he sells you falls apart.

If you elect *not* to buy this policy, you have no guarantee at all. And when you buy the car, you have to sign the FTC sticker, acknowledging that you are buying the car absolutely AS-IS. If the car comes apart at the seams as you leave the lot, it's your problem, and you can't expect the dealer to help.

The whole thing adds up to more profit for the dealer. Either you buy an expensive optional warranty (read: insurance policy) on which the dealer makes a handsome profit, or you sign an "as-is" form which effectively assures you no legal recourse even if you were sold a lemon intentionally.

Before the FTC sticker appeared on the scene, you could purchase a car from a reasonable and reputable dealer and safely assume that he was not trying to unload a can of worms on you. If something drastic did happen to that car before you made it a mile down the road, the dealer would usually help. And indeed, that was often the case.

An Example

For example, Nancy just signed the papers on a nice-looking, three-year-old car. Ken, Nancy's reasonable dealer, gave her the keys, and she proudly headed home. A few miles from the dealership, there was a loud clang and the rear wheels locked up. Nancy's dealer truly had no idea that the car was going to break. Had he driven it home that day, he would have been no less surprised. Fortunately for Nancy, Ken was a dealer who valued his reputation and her repeat business and he repaired the car.

"Reputation" is the operative word here. For too many dealers, the bottom line is more important than repeat business or any kind of good will. Yet there are several ways in which Nancy's case might have been handled.

If she had bought the car at the used-car lot of a new-car dealership, a common approach would be the dealer's offer to fix the car at "his cost," meaning that he would charge Nancy his "in house" costs, which have a generous profit margin factored into them. It also means that Nancy could probably have the car repaired at any independent garage for a lot less.

Some dealers might elect to let her return the car, as long as she traded it for another from their inventory. This would get Nancy off the hook for the lemon and give the dealer a chance to recover the repair costs in the profit on another sale, particularly if he can do some creative selling on the replacement car.

But now that the used-car industry has the infamous FTC sticker, even a reputable dealer can, with a clear conscience, tell his customer, "It's your problem." After all, if you choose to not take advantage of the "warranty" he offers (to sell) you, you *will* sign a form by which you agree that you are buying the car "as is." You now have no grounds to even take the dealer to court, because the judge would toss it out as soon as the dealer presented the "as is" clause that you signed.

Believe it or not, the exact wording on the FTC sticker is, "You will pay all costs for any repairs. The dealer assumes no responsibility for any repairs *regardless of any oral statements* [made] about the vehicle." (My emphasis.) So the dealer can tell you, "Oh, I have to put that form on the car to satisfy the Feds. Not to worry, though, we stand behind every car we sell. Trust me, I'm a dealer."

If the car breaks down the day after the sale, he is legally off the hook because you signed the FTC sticker. After all, *the form advised you not to listen to the dealer.* It stated that what he said didn't mean a thing.

The Federal Trade Commission assumes that the dealer is a liar. And the Federal Trade Commission calls this "consumer protection."

Summary

The last word? When you buy a car from a dealer, unless you can get him to fill in the "warranty" section of the FTC sticker with the details of his own warranty and the written version of any verbal promises he made, *you have no warranty*.

Since the law upholds the dealer's right to lie to you, he cannot be held liable for *any* verbal statement he makes to you.

You shouldn't consider buying a car marked "AS IS-NO WARRANTY" unless you are prepared to take care of any repairs yourself. Under these circumstances, you should get a great price on the car or be very sure of its satisfactory condition.

You'll learn all about warranties in Chapter 10 and how to make sure you're buying a good car in Chapters 14 through 16. Buying a good car in the first place is the best warranty there is!

WARRANTIES

New-car factory warranties have been improving in the last several years and manufacturers use them as competitive selling points. Most are limited, meaning that not everything is covered by the manufacturer; what *is* covered, is covered only under certain conditions.

Coverage varies from one year or 12,000 miles to five years or 50,000 miles or more and some have no mileage limits. Some offer different terms for different things: 24 months or 24,000 miles on most of the car; five years or 50,000 miles on the drive train; six years or 60,000 miles on body rust-through, as examples. Factory warranties are included in the selling price of the car.

Extended warranties, sold through auto dealers and backed by outside companies, are essentially insurance policies. You buy an extended warranty if you're the kind of person who assumes you'll have trouble while you own the car. Cost and *terms*--exactly what is covered, how, and for how long--determine how good a policy is.

Dealers are eager to offer these warranties because they profit greatly on the sale of each policy. As much as half of the cost of the warranty goes directly into the dealer's pocket. Because most people don't keep cars long enough to benefit from the warranty, insurance companies offer extended warranties eagerly. If they were not profitable to the insurer, the warranties would not be available.

The longer the term and more extensive the coverage, the more an extended warranty profits the dealer. The only way to come out ahead when buying an extended warranty is to keep the car for the length of that warranty and hope for a major failure. Not a happy thought!

Do you Really Need a Warranty?

Consider the last time you bought a used car with relatively few miles on it. Did you have any major problems with it? Probably not. As a dealer who has had access to many cars, I cannot remember *ever* having had any major mechanical problems on any car with less than 50,000 miles on it. Matter of fact, of all the cars I've sold to friends, relatives and their referrals (regardless of the miles on the cars), I've *never* been informed of a major problem.

Nearly any car that has had reasonable care and has less than fifty-thousand miles on it will run just fine with no problems far longer than most warranties cover. Certainly, there are exceptions but they are rare. If you buy a car using the information in this guide, your purchase will not be one of the exceptions.

A story

Here's a classic story: my sister and her husband bought one of the exceptions! It was a ten-year-old, full-size Ford wagon loaded with options.

They bought it in Canada, and unfortunately, I didn't get to look at it before they paid over $4000 for this tired, 140,000 mile turkey. The dealer convinced them that the miles were correct at the 40,000 (converted from kilometers) showing on the odometer.

It took me only a five-minute cursory examination to determine that the miles were "over" (the odometer had passed 100,000 and had started over). All the indicators were there: the upholstery and carpets showed more wear than they would have in 40,000 miles of use, the rubber brake-pedal cover was worn through to the metal in places and every cosmetic detail of the car showed lots of wear. Even if the car really had gone only the indicated miles, the wear and tear would have ruled it out as a likely candidate for purchase.

Then I looked under the hood. The transmission fluid smelled distinctly burned. Ford C-6 transmissions do not show burned fluid (bad clutches) at 40,000 miles; however, they often do at 140,000 miles. The air-conditioning compressor was making some pretty awful noises. Again, a clear symptom of lots of miles. These compressors sometimes need an overhaul, or at least bearings, at 80,000+ miles, but never at 40,000.

The engine also sounded tired. Big V-8 engines with low mileage and in good shape are very quiet. This one made lots of mechanical noise. Pulling the pcv (positive crankcase ventilation) valve out of the valve cover revealed way too much smoke (any is too much for a 40,000 mile car).

It had also obviously suffered from a poorly-repaired, major rear-end collision at some point in its history. And, although evidence of improperly-repaired major collision damage is no indication of the mileage of a car, it was certainly *another* clear reason to reject it.

The first trip taken in this car cost its proud new owners about $1000 in repairs. The air-conditioning compressor froze up, the catalytic converter plugged up and almost caught the car on fire, and there were other minor problems as well. Then the alternator went out.

A few months later, someone sold them yet another $120 alternator, claiming that whoever had sold them the last one had installed the wrong unit. They spent hundreds on the cooling system, which still overheats, and shelled out an amazing $900 to get the transmission overhauled. They are financially buried in the car and will probably put another $1000+ into it when the inevitable engine failure occurs. Or get rid of it. But when you have already poured about $8000 into a $1500 car, that's a tough decision.

This car certainly qualified as an exception. But it would have been easy to avoid the whole experience. That is what this book is all about: selecting a car that *doesn't need* a mechanical-failure insurance policy.

Buying one of the insurance policies offered by the dealers is rarely a good idea. In the first place, these policies are not offered on any cars which the dealer doesn't feel pretty sure about. (The company for whom the dealer is an agent will terminate any dealer who habitually sells cars that result in claims against the company.)

In the second place, the policies are expensive. You would have to suffer a major failure to break even on the price of the policy. Yes, it happens occasionally, but if it happened often enough to make the policy a good value, the policies would not be available. Insurance companies, selling the policies through auto dealers, are making a fortune on them. And the dealers' commissions are outrageous. You would do better to place the price of the extended warranty in a savings account and let it collect interest. Then, if you ever do need a repair, you'll have enough there to cover it.

Of hundreds of cars I've bought and sold over the years, many with over a hundred thousand miles, I've had *one* major problem. That was a bad transmission on a Chevy Citation, and had I paid better attention when checking out the car, I wouldn't have had even that one. (In my test drive, I didn't notice that reverse was slipping because I never had to back up.)

The chances of a major mechanical failure on any late model car which passes the tests outlined in this book are near zero.

Summary

Buying a new car because of the warranty sounds attractive until you consider how much more you're paying for the new car (than for a used one), and that in many cases, you will have to have all of your scheduled maintenance done by an authorized dealer. Dealer repairs and maintenance are almost always more costly than those done at independent garages.

If you are tempted to buy an "optional warranty" with the purchase of a used car, read the fine print! Find out exactly what it does and does not cover, and for how long.

Most optional warranties are just insurance policies, and the dealer makes a substantial profit whenever he sells one. They are never offered on cars that the dealer thinks are likely to need them.

If you select your car using the criteria in this book, an optional warranty is rarely a good investment. A major mechanical failure on any well-selected car is unlikely.

INSURANCE

Do you know anybody who ever felt they got a fair shake from their insurance company? Well, here's some info about what *can* occur, and some ways to make sure it'll never happen to you. One of the classic insurance ripoffs follows.

Drift back, if you will ... It is 1989, and you just bought yourself a brand new, top-of-the-line Honda Accord with all the toys. Of course, you told your insurance agent about your new car, and of course you bought full coverage insurance.

When you winced at the rate he quoted you for collision insurance, the agent patiently explained that the reason for the high premium is that the cost of repairing collision damage on a brand new, expensive car like yours is simply astronomical, and that your premium has to reflect this. The cost for your coverage was right there on the rate schedule, and that is what you had to pay.

So you paid. Then, for the next several years, you paid some more. Every six months, when the renewal came up, you paid again. The premium even went up once or twice during the last few years, right? But the old Honda was such a wonderful car, you decided when the speedometer logged 100,000 miles that you would just keep it until it would go no more.

Now, let's drift a few years into the future. It is now 1998. One dark night as you are driving home on icy streets, you lose control and the car skids into a retaining wall. Not hard enough to hurt anyone, but certainly hard enough to pretty much wipe out the pretty front end of your still-beautiful Accord.

You call your insurance agent, the one who has been faithfully renewing your collision policy for the last *nine years*. He tells you that he'll have an adjuster out there in the morning to appraise the damage.

The next morning the adjuster comes out to look at the car, walks around it slowly, shakes his head, and writes on his estimate form, "Cost of repairs exceeds value of car. TOTAL LOSS." He tells you that this old car isn't even in the book any more, but even though it has almost a hundred thousand miles on it, he'll be good to you and allow you twelve hundred dollars on it . . . Your nice insurance agent never bothered to remind you that it didn't make much sense to pay those collision premiums on that old car any more, did he?

This kind of overcharging can be avoided by reviewing your policy from year to year to make sure that what you paid for last year still applies. It doesn't cost as much to repair a five-year-old car as it did when it was brand new. And there comes a point in the life of most cars when expensive collision insurance is no longer cost-effective.

Many agents gloss over loopholes which allow the insurer to get out of paying a claim. Others, those who are responsible to their clients, take great pains to make certain that you're aware of all of possible loopholes. Ask for referrals!

By the way, the preceding scenario actually happened. Only it was Dad's Oldsmobile. When the Oldsmobile was involved in a major accident, the adjuster told Dad that since the car was so old, the company was not about to pay to have it fixed like new *even though for all those years, he had been paying for insurance for that very reason: to repair the car to the condition it was in before it was damaged.*

Watch Out for This One!

Another unethical practice which some insurance companies are running goes like this. If a car is involved in an accident, the adjuster will not allow the repair shop to use new factory parts if there are any cheap forgeries available.

These aftermarket imitations include most bolt-on sheet metal, such as fenders, hoods, some doors, bumpers and a lot of plastic parts, such as headlight moldings and grilles. (We'll refer to "aftermarket" parts a number of times in this discussion. "Aftermarket" means that the part is a copy of the original manufacturer's part, and it is made by someone other than the original manufacturer.) The quality control on most of these parts is a joke--ask any autobody repairman. The fenders don't fit, the character lines don't match, sometimes the installing technician even has to drill new bolt holes because the original ones were all in the wrong places. Hoods are wavy and don't fit up to the fenders.

While it might be excusable to use these inferior parts in the repairs of a six- or eight-year-old beater, to expect the owner of a nearly-new car (or an old car that has been carefully maintained) to settle for having her car repaired(?) with junk parts is unconscionable. It is particularly unforgivable after the owner has paid a lot of money each year for collision premiums on a policy which promises that the car will be properly repaired.

Premiums are supposed to be based upon what it costs to fix the car correctly (remember how the insurance salesman justified the high cost?). For the insurance company to declare, after a claim is filed, that they will use only cheap imitation parts is just plain crooked.

There are several other areas where the insurer might attempt to cut these kinds of corners in their never-ending quest for bottom-line, make-every-penny-count bookkeeping. One is on refinishing collision damage.

You know those beautiful, clear-coated glamour finishes that look so good on most of the newer cars? Well, the ONLY way that these finishes can be properly matched in a repair job is to use a two-stage (and on some newer cars, three-stage) system similar to the one with which the car was originally finished. A base-coat of color must be applied first, followed by the subsequent clear-coats. Very labor-intensive, and the materials cost a bunch.

Many insurance adjusters simply deny these charges on the shop estimate. They tell the shop that the company will pay only for a standard single-stage paint repair and, if the insured wants it done right, that he'll have to pay the difference, *even though the premium was based upon the cost of properly repairing the car.*

Even if a single-stage paint repair looks acceptable at the time it is done, it won't for long; the single-stage paints, particularly in the light metallic shades, do not last as long as the two- or three-stage paint jobs. The insurance companies are clearly cheating their customers out of millions of dollars every year.

The insurance company has effectively depreciated your car by hundreds of dollars, sometimes thousands; it now looks like a rebuilt wreck. So what? *They* saved a few bucks.

How about those plastic-covered bumpers on all the newer cars? Most insurance companies stipulate that the covers have to be repaired, not replaced, when damaged. It takes a certain amount of skill and craftsmanship to do an acceptable repair on a plastic bumper. In most cases, the "repair" will be quite apparent, and you, the customer will just have to live with it.

Protect Yourself

One way you have to protect yourself against this common practice of thievery is to insist that your collision policy contains language which clearly spells out that in the event of a claim for repairs on your car, only new, factory parts will be used; and that the shop, not the adjuster, will decide which parts need to be replaced rather than repaired.

Another step in the right direction is to go to a few body shops in your area and ask which insurance companies will allow the use of new parts and which ones won't, which insurers will allow the job to be done right, and which ones send out adjusters to chisel away at an estimate until there is hardly anything left.

Practices vary from place to place and from company to company. There *are* insurers and claims adjusters who will treat you fairly in the event of a loss. Ask for referrals!

Hanging on the office wall in most body shops is a sign spelling out the *law* that *prohibits* an insurance company or an agent of that company to tell you where to have your car fixed in the event of an accident. This law is largely ignored by many insurance adjusters and agents. Yet many people are hard to convince that they have the right to decide where their cars will be repaired.

One woman, one of my son's teachers, came to me in tears, asking if she really had to take her car to a particular shop with a reputation for terrible repair work. Her insurance agent had intimidated her until she felt that if she tried to take her car elsewhere, the insurance company wouldn't pay the claim at all.

I couldn't convince her otherwise. The agent had done her job well; she had also received her usual kickback from the shop for sending the work there. All the shop-owners in town knew of this agent and her intimidating practices, but she stayed in business and flourished. All it would have taken to stop her is informed consumers.

Kickbacks and other favors are common between repair shops and insurance people, as are other sorts of hanky-panky.

Another Story

A two-week-old Flashy Spendymobile just slid off an icy road damaging the front bumper, right front fender and door. The car was towed to Archie's Body Shop. Archie looked it over, drooling. He'd been looking for a Spendymobile for a special customer. The damage on the Flashy looked awful but was actually minor: there was no structural damage; only bolt-on parts needed to be replaced. The car could easily have been repaired to as-new condition.

When Jonathan the adjuster, Archie's buddy for years, came in to examine the car, Archie told him it was worth three hundred to him if the estimate got written up showing the car as a total loss. Since nobody else from the insurance company would look at the car, Jonathan had a free hand in writing up the damage report.

So he described the damage as far in excess of what it really was. He listed on his report the "salvage value" of the car, which Archie found an inviting price and eagerly paid. Jonathan got his three bills, the owner got a fair cash settlement for a new car, Archie got a good deal, and all the folks paying enormous premiums got screwed. Again.

The above scenario is becoming more difficult to pull off because most "totaled" cars now get shipped to salvage pools to be sold at auction. The people who run the salvage pools are now in position to siphon off the cream of what comes in.

Not that *all* salvage-pool operators are crooked, but every time a deal is made that allows an individual to obtain favors-- where one person is paying off another to see that he gets something he's not entitled to--premiums go up.

Here's an important tip: *If you ever need the services of a body shop, remember that the choice of shops is yours and yours alone. By law, the insurance company and/or* its agents and adjusters can't even <u>recommend</u> a shop, much less insist on one.

If the shop you choose writes an estimate of $1500 and your adjuster tells you that "his" shop will do the job for $500 less, so that's all the insurance company will pay, you do not have to accept this.

In the first place, there is no such thing as "his" shop. Even in the unlikely instance that the agent simply refers to the shop as "his" because of exemplary work at reasonable prices, it's still a good bet to steer away from the shop of his choice. The odds are in favor of there being more to it than that.

You have the option of going to as many shops as you want for estimates. (You aren't *required* to go to any at all. More on this later.) And if you find that all of the other estimates fall between $1300 and $1700, there is a good reason to assume that there is something wrong with the $1000 bid from your agent's favorite shop. If "his" shop will do the job for a lot less than *anyone* else will (and give your man a kickback besides), something's wrong. The difference will show up in the quality of the repair job.

Another tip: If the agent won't accept the lowest bid from the shops you contacted, tell him that you are going to ask the insurance commissioner if what he's doing is legal. If that doesn't get his attention, call your state's insurance commissioner, who is listed in the yellow pages under the "State Offices" listings. Otherwise, the shop gets a job, the agent gets a kickback, and you get burned.

Here's how the "normal" process of getting estimates works: You spend your time driving your damaged car all over town to get three estimates. You send them to the insurance company and they promptly toss all but the lowest one. Then they direct you to leave your car at that shop and make an appointment for the car to be examined by their adjuster. He will write yet another estimate, cutting all the corners he can, chiseling the lowest estimate down to the point where the shop can barely afford to take the job. The bottom line is that the insurance adjuster is the one who writes the estimate that decides what the company will pay, so why bother getting all the other estimates? Just take the car to the shop of your choice and tell the company that's where the car will be repaired. If the company balks, call your State Insurance Commissioner.

Of course all of this presumes that you're the kind of woman who is willing to stand up for your rights. Sometimes it takes a little extra assertiveness to pull it off, and if you are uncomfortable with this, just take it as far as what feels good to you. Perhaps ask a friend for some help. It's important to know what your rights are!

If your car is damaged to the point where it cannot be driven around to other shops for estimates, fret not. The other shops will come to you. Go to the shop of your choice and tell their estimator where the car is. In most cases, he will be glad to go examine your car and write an estimate.

Most adjusters and agents will use your urgent need for the return of your car as leverage to get their way. Let them know that you don't care how long it takes to resolve the estimate-for-repairs situation even if that's not the case. As soon as an unscrupulous adjuster knows that you are desperate to get your car back, he knows that if he slows things down dramatically enough, you will settle for anything he offers.

Some insurance companies will pay for a rental car while yours is being repaired, but even some of those won't start paying until the repair price is settled and the car is in the shop that's going to repair it.

Sounds pretty grim, doesn't it? Well, rest assured that it is often worse than it sounds. We are describing here only the up-front, lightweight swindles that are clearly visible to the public. The deeper you dig, the worse it gets.

Contrary to the assertions of many in the insurance business, you *do* have rights. And there *are* honest people in the business; not all are on the "take." The insurance agents selling the policies have to deal with the knowledge that the companies they represent rarely deliver what they promise.

Summary

Shop around for several quotes on your auto insurance; rates vary a lot. When deciding whether or not to buy collision insurance, use statistics just like the insurance companies do. When's the last time you've ever needed collision insurance? Have you ever? How old is the car and what's it worth? If you're driving a $2000 car and your insurer wants $400 a year for collision coverage, this is not a good deal. It means that every five years, you've paid for the entire value of your car. And that doesn't even take into account depreciation. If the car was worth $2000 five years ago, it isn't any more!

Optional collision insurance (*your* option) is one of the benefits of owning your car free and clear. If it is financed, you have no choice; you *have to* buy the insurance. When you figure out that extra cost and add it to the finance charges, it gets tempting to go buy a car you can afford to pay cash for!

Read the fine print (like nobody ever does!) before you sign any policy or application. Look at the language and make sure you are *clear* about what it actually says.

Ask for referrals. Talk to your friends, business associates, or co-workers and ask for recommendations for insurance agents with whom they've had satisfactory dealings. If the need ever arises, do the same for body shops. When you do decide on a potential repair shop, ask to see a job or two that they've just completed.

Always remember that where you go to have insurance work done is *your* choice, not the insurance company's. The adjuster will ask you to provide several estimates, and you don't even need to do that.

The work generally gets done to the adjuster's estimate, not to the one written by any of the shops, so why bother?

Remember that many adjusters are actually trained to manipulate you into a quick/low settlement. If you ever get to the frustration level where you feel you're not in control, don't sign anything! Take a break, step back from the situation and try to look at the whole picture. And if you feel that you're being treated unfairly, don't hesitate to call your state insurance commissioner!

FINANCING

If you look to this chapter for tricks on how to buy the most car with the least money down, you'll be disappointed! Ideally, we should all pay cash for our cars. If you can save enough money beforehand and then buy a car which you can afford, you eliminate interest as an expense of car ownership. But since paying cash is often impossible if not un-American, you may have to find some kind of reasonable financing. Here's how.

About the only way to buy a car with borrowed money without losing in the process is to buy a special-interest car that will appreciate in value over the years (See Chapter 5). For the rest of us who just want to buy a regular, garden-variety, late-model car and drive it until we either tire of it or wear it out (not likely), the first and most important rule of thumb is: *never borrow so much of the price of the car that its value will depreciate faster than the loan gets paid down!* This may seem obvious, but we'll get into some of the tricks used by dealers that get uninformed car-buyers into exactly this kind of trouble.

"Zero Down!"

An easy way to fall into a trap is to listen to the "Zero Down" ads. A large proportion of the payments on a new loan go to interest, meaning that very little of the payment is actually reducing the amount you owe on the car. If you buy a new car with "zero down," the car will depreciate several thousand dollars before you get it home and you'll still owe the full price on it. Not a good start. But then, that's only one of the many reasons to avoid buying a new car!

There's a popular scam (one among many) to lure people into new-car showrooms. It allows you to make a tiny, say $100, down-payment, and to make only half-payments for the first year of a five-year contract. As of the thirteenth month, the full payments commence.

The deal sounds great to a lot of optimists who figure they probably won't keep the car for more than about a year anyway and to dreamers who are counting on a sizable raise; it seems a lifesaver to those who can never seem to save up a down payment.

What gets buyers into trouble is that those half-payments often don't even pay the interest on the loan, much less any principal. At the end of one year, they could well *owe more on the car than they had originally paid for it!*

If, at the end of the first year (or after a few months of making the now-double payments on the now no-longer-new-and-exciting car) the optimist decides that she would like to be relieved of her burden, she will find out that there is no way out of her predicament. The car has depreciated down to $2000 less than she owes on it.

She now realizes what she's gotten herself into. Her options? Make another four years of payments.

Or sell the car and get a personal loan for the $2000 difference between what she can get for it and what she owes on it. Then she gets to pay off the $2000 for a car she doesn't even have any more. Or she can allow the car to be repossessed.

If she chooses repossession, she will be sued for the difference between what the lending institution sells the car for (often less than it's worth) and the outstanding balance on the loan. At the very least, she'll have a hard time ever getting another loan.

Another reason to avoid the teensy down-payment temptation is that in the unlikely event your car should ever be totalled in an accident, the insurance company will pay only what they interpret the "Blue Book" value of the car to be. If that happens to be less than what you still owe on the car, you will have to pay the difference, even though there is no more car!

Get Your Own Financing!

The most important point we can make regarding financing of cars is this: *secure your own financing!* Dealer financing always costs more.

In the first place, the dealer makes a profit from your transaction with the lender, meaning that you could get the financing cheaper elsewhere. In the second and more significant place, allowing the dealer to bring financing into the transaction gives him the opportunity for more manipulations, and he is well trained in the fine art of the manipulation of figures. It is in the juggling of financing figures that many buyers pay up to thousands of dollars more for a car than was implied verbally by the dealer. Unless you are unusually skilled in math, some of these manipulations are very difficult to detect.

There *are* a few legitimate reasons to go with dealer financing. If you are a student or just have no prior credit history, or if you have a problem credit-history, dealer financing may accommodate you when the other sources will not. The important things to keep in mind here are to keep the loan down to a very manageable amount and make your payments right on schedule. That way, this loan can be the foundation for your future credit. Just be very careful, and take the time to read all the fine print. Multiply the number of payments by the amount of each payment and make sure that you come out with the same figure as is shown on your sales agreement.

Arrange Your Financing Beforehand.

Always be prepared to pay cash for your car, regardless of where you get the money. Arrange your financing before you go shopping.

Did you know that you can get a financing commitment from your bank or credit union before you even select a car? Actually, most lenders would *prefer* that you come to them before you go shopping. That way you can discuss things like credit limits, repayment schedules and interest rates at your leisure, instead of after the car has been chosen, when bad judgment under pressure is more likely.

Tell your lender that you will be buying a car, about how much you plan to budget for the purchase, and how much of that you need to borrow. Ask for a commitment for that amount, so that when you go shopping you will be able to deal for a cash sale, putting you in position for a more favorable transaction.

If you have lending options, such as several banks or a credit union, ask for the interest rate from each. They do vary. Many lenders will offer a lower interest rate on a new-car purchase than on a used car. Forget it! Factor in the incredible instant depreciation of new cars while you try to figure out how much interest you would save.

Tax-Deductible Auto Loans

Another way to finance a car is with a loan on your house. As with a home-improvement loan, the paperwork is usually fairly simple. There are several distinct advantages to this option. First, the interest on a loan on your home is tax-deductible, while the interest on an auto loan is not. Then there's the insurance thing. If the car isn't used as collateral, there will be no requirement to buy expensive collision insurance. (This is *not* a recommendation to do without collision insurance. This financing option just allows you to decide for yourself whether or not to buy it.) Keeping the title of the car unencumbered also gives you the freedom to replace the car without having to go through some more financing red tape. Do the arithmetic to see which way is the most cost-effective for you. For many people, the tax advantage is significant.

OK, but what about those irresistible "4.9% APR" interest rates offered on new cars? Dealers often advertise temptingly low interest rates, *especially* on new cars. These ads usually also contain language (in fine print) spelling out the fact that you can get *either* the low interest rate *or* the also-offered rebate, but not both. The rebate, together with your own financing, is usually the better deal.

Recently, there's been a lot of discussion on the misleading nature of those supposed low-interest loans. What actually happens is that the interest is figured into the price of the car. Not only that, these loans are often available only on selected cars, usually those the dealer has a surplus of. None of the usual rebates or other incentives are offered, and you don't qualify unless you pay the full manufacturer's suggested list price (MSRP). The MSRP has a generous margin figured into it that allows the dealer all sorts of room. I don't recall ever hearing of anybody actually paying MSRP on a new car.

You can almost always do better (Do the math!) than the "low interest loan" by going to your bank or credit union for a conventional eight or 9 percent loan and then driving a better bargain with the dealer for a cash sale.

New vs. Used (Again)

As an incentive to buy new rather than used, dealers often offer new-car financing interest at rates well below those that a bank will allow on a used-car purchase.

Consider Iris. A $12,000 price tag attracted her to a possible new-car purchase because the interest rate was only 9%, as opposed to the 12% she would have to pay at her bank if she bought a $6000 used car.

She was going to use her old car as the whole down payment, so she'd be financing $5000 on the used car, or $10,000 on the new one, since they were going to give her "$2000!" for her clunker (the one that's actually worth $1000), on the new ride. The used car, at 12% on a 36-month note would cost about $978 in interest with the payments at $166/month.

The new car, financed for 48 months at 9%, would cost $1944 in interest; the monthly payments would be $249. Stretched out to 60 months, the payments would drop to $208/month but the interest would climb to $2455 over the life of the contract. The used car would end up costing her a total of

$6978; the new one, $13,944 on the shorter of the two contracts.

If she lives in a state that charges 6% sales tax, she can add another $360 to the used car and $777 to the new one. Many states charge license fees based upon the selling price or book value of the car, imposing yet another penalty for buying the more expensive car. And that doesn't include the much steeper insurance premiums for the new car.

For someone who had decided rationally to stay within a $6000 budget, the new car should never have been a consideration.

The used car, a week after purchase, is still worth its purchase price. The new car, *which is a used car as soon as she signs the papers,* will be worth--if she's lucky--$3000 less than its purchase price. If she adds that $3000 in depreciation to the greater interest cost of the cheaper-to-finance new car, "cheaper" loses much of its meaning.

Summary:
    1. Never allow a dealer to finance your car.
    2. Get your own financing, and shop around for that. Rates, fees and conditions vary a lot from one lender to another. It always pays to compare.

3. Get your financing commitment before you go shopping. That way you'll already know what the costs will be and how much money you have to work with and you'll be in a much better bargaining position as a "cash customer."

4. Those super-low-interest loans advertised by many dealers are not what they appear to be. They are available only on selected cars (the ones the dealer selects) and are available instead of the advertised rebates or other incentives. They are carefully figured into the price of the car and all other factors of the sale, and in the end will cost you more than outside financing at a higher rate.

PLANNED OBSOLESCENCE

Planned obsolescence is not a new idea. You've all had experiences with appliances that magically fall apart on the expiration date of their warranties. But not all obsolescence deals with wear. Much of it is planned into the *appearance* of the things we buy.

Are you old enough to remember the early fifties when Chevrolet dazzled the public with its brand new line of super-deluxe cars called *Bel Air*?

Everybody had to have one. Then in 1958 they dropped the Bel Air's status a notch by introducing the *Impala*. If you still had a Bel Air in your driveway in 1958, you obviously were on some kind of an embarrassing budget because the Impala was the way to go.

And so it went. The *Caprice*. Then the *Caprice Classic*. Every few years the top-of-the-line models got one-upped by another new *name*.

Now, when prospective buyers go to look at the new cars on the showroom floors or at the gala annual auto shows, most of the cars aren't new at all. They certainly aren't the newest thing the industry could offer. The really new stuff, which is on the drawing boards *right now*, will not show up on the showroom floor for years. The whole game is a carefully thought-out scheme of long-term, planned obsolescence.

Want some examples of this standard, industry-wide practice? One popular Japanese automaker's favorite method is to introduce a brand-new, high-dollar sports model in, let's say, 1995.

It was a new number, so all the people who were obsessed with owning what is HOT! rushed to buy one. They hardly noticed that although these new cars looked really great, they were available in only three colors and only with a rather drab, grey interior. Didn't matter. Trend setters told themselves, "I would really rather have it in blue with a black interior but this is such a great-looking car and it's NEW. What the heck?" They bought it anyway.

But what happened in '96? The same car, which was no longer new, appeared on the market in the dazzling array of colors that were available on *every* model of that maker's *other* cars in '95. It was now available with all the interior color options, too. As far as the manufacturer was concerned, they had introduced another "new" car. They did it by intentionally withholding colors from the first model that were available on the rest of their whole product line. Their experience had shown that a predictable number of people would buy the new car in basic grey, just because it was "new." When that market dried up, they offered the full color line and opened their doors to a whole new arena of (well-programmed) buyers.

The system works, and it works well. A lot of the people who bought the drab '95 model rationalized dropping another few thousand dollars in '96 to buy the same car in the colors they would have liked--and which should have been available--in the first place.

A Plan for Obsolescence

Here's another one. A little dated, but it's a good, clear example or standard industry practice. Subaru built a wonderful little front- or four-wheel-drive vehicle, a humble little car when first presented in the middle seventies. In 1980 the company introduced their first really nice-looking version of that car. The new line included a four-door sedan, a great-looking two-door hardtop, a wagon and a hatchback. But four-wheel drive was available only in the hatchback and wagon.

After a couple of years, Subaru enthusiasts started saying it would be nice if the other models also came in a 4x4 version. But, no. All the folks who needed four-wheel drive and would have jumped at a hardtop or sedan had to settle for the wagon or hatchback.

Then in 1984, Subaru did it! They made their public ecstatic with the introduction of 4x4 hardtops and 4x4 sedans. Again, a lot of buyers who had settled for their second choices in 1983 jumped in and bought yet another new car in 1984, purely in response to Subaru's carefully mapped-out strategy.

What strategy?

1984 was the last year of the then-current body style. In 1985 Subaru introduced another completely "new" line of cars. For an automaker to sell the last year's run of an old body style while many are willing to wait for the new one, a gimmick is needed. Subaru engineered the 1984 gimmick into their then-new line in 1980.

If you peek underneath the first hardtops and sedans that Subaru produced in 1980, you will see all of the attachment points and access holes for mounting the mechanical 4x4 components. Those cars were designed from the beginning for installation of four-wheel-drive. Subaru merely waited until just the right time, the last year of production of that body design, to "introduce" a feature which was *actually ready* since the beginning. This sales-boosting technique for a last-year model run is not unique to Subaru. Standard industry practice demands a powerful gimmick for the last year of a model run.

More often than not, this is accomplished with "special edition models," most of which are identical to last year's models, except for the addition of some new striping, special moldings, perhaps an interior unique to this model, a package of accessories included as "standard," maybe even a turbocharger. But the end result is still the old car, the last of the model-year run, once more disguised as something new.

Another One

Another gimmick that works every time is with "new" pickups. In the first model year, you'll rarely see an "extended cab" version. And even though the designs are done and maybe the tooling is already in place, the manufacturer will withhold the special model, which they know is a good seller, until the buyers who would rather have had the extended-cab settle for the regular-cab version. These buyers are now already programmed to upgrade as soon as the one they really want appears.

Another scheme of planned obsolescence is the purposeful manufacture of a product in such a way that it starts to look shoddy long before it begins to actually wear out or perform poorly, motivating its owner to seek "new" once again.

For example, look at the "chrome" trim on and around the dashboards of most cars built within the last ten years. Examine all of the edges and ridges that look like chrome, or did when the car was new. Chances are, the chrome-like substance is in good shape only where it never gets touched.

This "chrome" is a plating process which leaves such a thin film of metal on the surface that normal wiping with household cleaners will remove it. That's on the expensive models. On the cheaper ones it's thin paint, which can also be wiped off . . . if it hasn't already worn off by the time you get it home.

If you can buy an inexpensive plastic kitchen gadget with a chrome finish that lasts for years without showing any wear, can it be accidental that the finish on exposed parts of your $18,000 car is so poor? The chrome was meant to glitter its way into your heart and wallet on the showroom floor and to disappear right before your eyes soon after the purchase.

Have you ever wondered whether it is simply coincidence that gas prices and car sizes take frequent inversely proportional roller-coaster rides?

Remember the sixties and seventies, when cars kept getting bigger and bigger? The ads kept telling you that the new Whooshmobile was a whole foot-and-a-half longer than the opposition's newest monster and how impressed all your neighbors would be if you had one in your driveway. Cars got bigger until they became absurd: vast expanses of gaudy-colored sheet metal, some were not unlike circus floats. The roller-coaster climbed up.

Gas prices started climbing, too. And climbing. It wasn't long before the car companies came to the rescue. Lucky consumers could suddenly trade in their whale-like cars on smaller ones and get better mileage. Only it wasn't that simple. The big old cars were safer, more comfortable, more powerful and obviously more expensive. After having reached that plateau, drivers were reluctant to come down.

But obsolescence can also be contrived by advertising. Enter Madison Avenue. Ads began to intimate that it was unfashionable to be seen in a big car. It soon became downright unacceptable. The used car market was turned upside down, with prices dropping out the bottom on full-size cars. It was amazing to see a two-year-old Pinto sell for more money at the wholesale dealers' auction than a same-year, full-sized, loaded Ford LTD! The roller-coaster swooped down.

About the time the auto industry had saturated the market with socially-acceptable teensy cars, gas prices started back down. And down. New ads declared that safety and comfort were certainly more important than trying to save a few pennies on gas. Mini-cars just weren't safe. Besides, the new, larger cars were getting better mileage than their previous generation.

Each model year saw the cars growing again. Each model year brought advertising which blatantly informed the car-buying public that the new car was more luxurious because it was nearly a foot longer than the one they claimed was the greatest thing on the road last year. The roller-coaster was on its way back up.

The same thing happened with diesel cars. About the time that the gas prices really started soaring, Detroit introduced the diesel option. In theory, driving a diesel-powered car would save a pile of money. GM sold thousands of them before people started to realize that their ill-conceived, converted-from-gas engines were coming apart at the seams.

Not all diesel engines were poorly built, and at the height of diesel's popularity, most automakers were offering diesel engines in most of their product lines. Then, through another amazing coincidence, just about the time that all the diesels they were going to sell were sold, the price of diesel fuel started going up until it cost as much as or more than gasoline! Who in his right mind was going to hang onto a smelly, gutless, unreliable, noisy diesel when he could drive a gas-engine car for the same money?

In today's auto market, a diesel engine is the kiss of death. At the auctions, when a diesel drives into the auction barn, almost everybody walks out. If a diesel car sells at all, it will usually bring half what the same unit would have sold for with a gas engine. And often the buyer is someone who will install a gas engine in the car and resell it at a comfortable profit.

The auto industry has the consumer well trained to respond to its every suggestion. And the billions of dollars spent each year on advertising are paying big dividends. Car ads are no longer selling cars; they are selling lifestyles. When is the last time you saw any technical details offered in a TV ad for a car? What you do see is beautiful people attracting more beautiful people with the cars they appear in.

Advertising and planned obsolescence work together as an effective team. America's merchandising system is based on these two premises, in the auto market and elsewhere.

"Different"

"Different" is an important operative in the world of planned obsolescence. Most "new" cars are not new at all. Just different. A few trim items may have changed, but just enough to let your friends know whether or not you still have last year's model.

This whole concept is emphasized every day in auto ads. They'll put on this super-expensive prime-time ad that tells you their new car is " . . . more powerful, quieter and handles better!" Than what? The whole point of the ad is to convince you that there's something out there that's better than what you've already got. They don't *say* that, but that's the clear implication, the subliminal message.

If anything can be learned from this discussion, it might be that buying a second-hand car in premium condition is a wise decision. If you are the slightest bit inclined to pay the enormous penalty necessary to own a new car just because you will then own something unique, be sure to read the chapter on "The Special-Interest Car." If a new car interests you because of the warranty, please read Chapter 10, "Warranties." And always keep in mind that the minute a new car leaves the showroom floor, it's just another used car.

Consider this: if you bought a new car today, drove it for a year, maintained it and kept it in perfect condition, wouldn't you still consider it your "new" car? What if for some reason you had to sell it right then? Wouldn't that car, having depreciated several thousands of dollars, be an excellent value to its next owner? Wouldn't it be an even better value now than it was to you as a new car? Think about that when you consider a new car!

Summary

The word "new," when applied to cars, doesn't have much more meaning than just *new to you*. There is little that is really new in any new car. If maximum miles per *dollar* are your concern, buying a new car *because it's something new* is not a good investment.

The concept of "new" having some special value in and of itself has been a brainchild of Madison Avenue psychologists for years, and it's worked very well on the American public. Just the word "NEW!" in an advertisement is enough to catch most people's attention right away.

Allowing yourself to fall into the "new is good" trap puts you on a dead-end street. Whatever you acquire that's new today will be old tomorrow and the new will once again become desirable. See Chapter 5, Special Interest Cars, for a delightful alternative to "new."

Check It Out: The Part That Shows

Are you ready to roll up your sleeves now? You've spent a lot of time doing constructive, objective reasoning about cars, right? You've kept in mind the role your emotions will play in the selection of your new (used) car, and you feel comfortable knowing that your decision will be based on good judgment. Well, mostly.

You've found a car that's just what you've been looking for, so now is the time to make sure that this is also the car you really want: a car that has received proper maintenance and is exactly what it appears to be. You don't want to end up with a carefully disguised lemon.

This part gets into some technical stuff that you may or may not want to deal with on your own. None of the techniques described here are beyond what you can handle, if you want to. You just need to pay close attention to some details; you don't have to be an auto-mechanic. If you don't feel up to it, take someone with you who is familiar with cars and how they work. (Not just somebody who *says* they are, either!)

Has it Been Wrecked?

Let's begin with the question you'll likely ask first, "Has it ever been wrecked?"

The body, paint, and general appearance of the car present its first impression. Most buyers have been programmed to reject a car automatically if they find out it has been wrecked.

Wrecks happen in many degrees. Just because a car has been "wrecked" does not necessarily mean that you should reject it. Some damaged cars can be repaired properly by the average body shop, and some shouldn't be repaired at all. If you are seriously considering buying a car that you know has had body damage beyond a minor scrape, it's a good idea to have it looked at by a professional.

The first and most obvious clue to body repairs is found in the paint that covers those repairs. If a car has been completely refinished, it is usually easy to tell. With few exceptions, most body shops are pretty sloppy at masking. This makes it easy to spot a repaint.

Repaints

When a car is painted at the factory, the body is devoid of all trim, moldings, glass, nameplates, bumpers, etc.

CLUE: *If you spot any body-color paint on any of these items, anywhere on the car, there has been some repainting done.*

On a complete repaint, this evidence is likely to be all over the car. Any areas that are difficult or time-consuming to mask, will generally have paint on them--at least along the edges closest to the body. Of course, the better the paint job, the neater the masking is likely to be. Even on the uncommonly well-masked car, lifting up the edges of any soft trim (rubber seals around glass and some moldings) will usually reveal the evidence you're looking for.

Slide a fingernail under the edges of soft trim here and there, and look for the telltale edge of new paint. Another product of sloppy masking, is overspray. Overspray is any paint that reached any place it wasn't supposed to go.

Open the doors and inspect along their inner edges. Look for body-color paint on the black rubber door-seal gasket. Look especially at the door jamb. It should show only clean, shiny, factory paint. If there is some fuzzy, dull paint showing around the edges of the jambs, there has been some repainting done. Open the trunk and look for the same thing. The black rubber gasket which seals the trunk lid to the body will have no body-color overspray on it unless there has been some carelessly-masked repainting done.

Now look under the hood: a classic area of sloppy or non-masking. Most cars have little rubber bumpers or pads along the inner edges of the fenders.

These pads are rattle- and vibration- dampers, and contact the hood when it is closed. There should be no paint on these parts, nor on any other rubber pieces or gaskets around the hood opening.

Some shops are so careless about engine compartment protection that the entire engine and everything else under the hood might be covered with a fine dusting of body color. If the car has a cowl screen (a panel, usually with slots or a grille of some sort to admit fresh air to the car's heating/cooling system, (between the back edge of the hood and the bottom of the windshield), look into the openings.

Cowl screens are time-consuming to mask or remove, and will often show evidence of repainting. If there is a screen or mesh panel visible through the openings in the cowl screen, it should have no body-color paint on it.

Another place that often gets overspray is tires and wheelwells. Wheelwells, the black inner-panels under the wheel-openings in the fenders, are difficult to mask.

Why is it so important to tell if a car has been repainted? We're not necessarily concerned about the paint job itself. What we're looking for is the *reason* that the car was painted. Often a car is painted after major collision or rust repairs, and that's what we're trying to smoke out here: why was it necessary to paint the car? This is especially significant on a car that's only a few years old. There's little reason to repaint a three- or even a ten-year-old car unless there was some damage somewhere. Sometimes, a car's original factory paint has a problem that necessitates a repaint, but that's the exception.

Spot Painting

"Spot painting" is the refinishing of a small area; just enough to cover the repair or replacement of a panel, such as a fender or door. Spot painting is a little harder to detect, because there isn't as much of it. Unless a spot job is very well done, it can be most easily seen by squatting down at the front or back of the car and looking carefully down the entire side, one panel at a time.

Look for any irregularities: something in one area that is not the same as the rest of the surface.

Just about any unrepaired car will have body panels which are smooth, shiny and uniform. If there has been a less-than-perfect repair made, that area will show small ripples in the body surface, and/or a different texture in the paint.

For example, if you catch a reflection in a piece of glass or a mirror, it will be perfectly smooth. If in the mirror, you see the reflection of an object with straight lines, the lines in the reflection will be straight as well. Few cars have finishes this smooth, but many come close.

The trick is to catch reflections. Move around so that as you look into the finish of the car, you can see the reflection of something--a tree, a house, whatever reflects in the surface of the car. Reflections should be similar everywhere on the car. If one particular area gives a dull or fuzzy reflection, or if straight lines reflect as wiggly, there's been a repair done. It sounds complicated, but once you see the first reflected object in the car's finish, the technique will become obvious and easy. This technique works especially well to find bodywork that's been done on the sides of cars. You'll have to squat down near the front or back of the car and just look down the side from one end to the other.

Another common tell-tale sign of bodywork is "sandscratch." This shows up as fine sanding marks in or under the paint, showing that preparation of the undercoats wasn't done properly. The sanding then shows through the finish.

Again, just because a car has had a minor fender-bender, it is not necessarily a candidate for rejection. What you are looking for is evidence of bodywork that will serve as clues to finding major repairs. Often, finding a simple thing like overspray or sloppy masking can prompt a more careful investigation which reveals serious hatchet-work where somebody thought nobody would look.

Panel Alignment

The more serious collision repairs, if poorly done, will usually reveal themselves in ill-fitting doors, hoods, and deck lids. Generally, you may assume that wherever you see a space between any two panels wider at one end than the other, something underneath is bent.

For example, if the space between the front door and the fender is an eighth of an inch wider at the top than it is at the bottom, something is wrong. They don't put them together at the factory that way. (With very few exceptions, that is.)

You will almost never find any foreign car with less-than-perfect panel alignment. Even bottom-of-the-line Japanese cars are impeccable in fit and finish. American auto manufacturers, unfortunately, are not quite as fussy about details.

CLUE: *The gaps between each two panels on cars should be the same width throughout the gap, and consistent from one panel to the next.*

If you find a vehicle with a space wider at one end than the other between the hood and the fender, or the fender and the door, or the door and the rear quarter panel, or anywhere else for that matter, there IS some structural damage hiding underneath. The ONLY reason for such a misalignment in panels is a misalignment of the structure which supports the external sheet metal.

Another place to look for panel misalignment is in the surfaces of the panels, relative to each other. For example, on a four-dour sedan, if the doors are flush at the top but the front door sticks out a quarter of an inch farther than the rear door at the bottom, something is seriously wrong. If this kind of misalignment appears in several places on the car, it is possibly a "repaired" rollover in which the entire body structure is still twisted.

The door-to-fender, door-to-door, and door-to-quarter panel alignment should be nearly perfect on just about any car that hasn't been wrecked. No panel will stick out from its neighboring panel at the top or bottom on a car that has not been crunched.

To speak of perfect alignments between body panels may seem nit-picky, but it is often this clue which reveals "rebuilt" totals that should never have been rebuilt, or at least should have been rebuilt by someone competent to do the job. A qualified craftsman with the right tools and adequate expertise can do amazing repairs to a bent and twisted car. Many seemingly-unrepairable wrecks can be repaired to as-new specifications.

The operative phrase here is "can be." Many wrecks are "repaired" just enough to disguise the damage: the car may look satisfactory to the untrained eye, but it can also be structurally unsound . . . and unsafe.

I've seen bent-frame cars where the error was so extreme that the body man loosened both doors on the damaged side, and adjusted them to average out the error down the whole side of the car. All of the spaces between each two panels were a little wider at the top than at the bottom, instead of having a glaring error all in one place.

Some kinds of bad bodywork don't matter much; they only look bad to the trained eye. But other bad bodywork can seriously compromise the safety of the vehicle. And all bad bodywork depreciates the value of a car.

Exactly what constitutes "bad" bodywork, anyway? When your car is involved in an accident, you take it to a body shop to be repaired. The goal of the repair people is to make the car look like it did before it was hurt. In other words, when the job is done, there should be no evidence of a repair having been made. If the "repair" is visible, it is unsatisfactory. Of course the exception to this is a repair made to a vehicle with oxidized or faded paint, or one already blessed with an edgy repaint job. But when dealing with a car that has the original finish in well-maintained condition, a visible repair is bad bodywork.

Check for rust!

If you live in a coastal area or anywhere where salting roads in winter is standard practice, rust-inspection is important. In these areas, any car advertised with "new paint" is suspect.

It's important to check for rust because to a car, rust is cancer. It spreads and destroys, and usually far beyond what's visible in any casual inspection. I've seen pretty decent looking cars that were so badly rusted underneath that they were unsafe do drive. It's nearly impossible to stop, too. On an especially valuable car, rust repairs are often made by completely removing the affected panels or parts and welding in replacements. Most shops do rust "repairs" by installing metal patches over the rusted areas, or by simply filling in them with body filler. Both ways are temporary fixes.

Lots of badly rusted cars that are in otherwise OK condition get sent to body shops for a quick patch-and-paint (by both dealers and private-parties). They'll look pretty good for a few months, and then the rust starts popping through everywhere, and soon, they'll look as bad as they did before. In almost all cases, rust-repairs are temporary and will rust through again in a few months.

If you suspect rust repairs, look at the bottom edges of doors, inside the front door-jambs, around the edge of the trunk opening and under the hood. Most rusted cars will be rusty under the hood, too. There will be rust everywhere; on just about every part made of steel. Cars with sunroofs often show signs of rust around the edges of the opening, and when the sunroof is opened (or better yet, removed), there will be evidence of rust down in the corners of the opening, especially where the drain holes are. Look for rust in the mechanism that operates the little air-deflector in the front of many sunroof openings, too.

Another likely place for rust to start showing is in the lower corners of any windows, particularly back windows.

Sloppy rust repairs usually appear as slightly lumpy surfaces, and if they were done long enough ago to already be failing, there will also be lots of little blisters. You're much better off buying an original (not repainted) car with a little *visible* rust, so that you know exactly where and how bad it is, than to buy one that has been "repaired" and take the sellers word for it.

If you live where the roads are salted, by all means check under the car, too. I've seen cars with major suspension-components nearly rusted through! Even if it isn't that bad, it's nearly impossible to service or repair a car when all the nuts and bolts underneath are rusted solid. Better to keep looking for that special car!

Some kinds of rust damage can be repaired. Verifiably *local* damage to fender-wells, trunk floors, and other structural areas that can be relatively easily removed and replaced without getting into major body surgery can be dealt with by a good body shop. It's still going to be expensive, though, and should only be considered if the car is worth the effort and you can't find a rust-free substitute.

Pay special attention to the driver's door when opening and closing it. It should give no indication of "dropping" when you open it, and when you close it gently, it should come naturally into place with no bumping or climbing of the latch mechanism. If the door seems to bump against or climb up on the latch when you close it, open it again and lift up on the outer end of the door to check the hinges. There should be almost no discernable movement here. If the hinges are worn, suspect that the car has seen mostly city-type, stop-and-go driving; the hardest kind of use on a car. If the hinges are worn on a low-mileage car, suspect that the odometer is not telling the truth!

Look Inside

The of a car can tell you volumes about the care it's received. What is your overall impression when you first look inside? Neat and clean? Clean but worn? Shabby and dirty?

It's been my experience that most people who never clean the interior of their cars don't bother with any other maintenance, either. I'll reject any car with a filthy interior for that reason. But how do you tell if the car you're looking at was just detailed and was filthy yesterday? Check the spots that are hard to clean. Pull apart places in the upholstery where cushions or seams come together and check for the grime that the detailer missed. Open the ash trays and glove box. Check around the edges. Look under the seats, too.

When checking the interior, sit in the back seat for a moment and look around. (Nobody ever does that!) Look up at the headliner (the ceiling covering). That's a place that a lot of people never notice until after they've owned the car for a while. Check the carpets, and be sure to look under any floormats. Pay particular attention to the carpet at the driver's heel position. That's where they usually break downs first.

Look at the brake and clutch pedals. How worn are they? If the car shows 50,000, expect some wear. If they're brand new, expect the car either has more than 50,000 miles on it, or it's been used for mostly stop-and-go driving. While on the subject of stop-and-go driving, check the left side of the driver's seat for the kind of wear that is likely from somebody having gotten in and out of the car about a bezillion times. That's another indication of lots of city driving, the worst kind.

Look carefully at the seats for seams that are loose and about to open up, and for cracked vinyl. These things may not look bad now, but if they're on the edge, they'll look shabby in a short while and they're expensive to fix. A well-maintained car shouldn't show any appreciable wear on the upholstery, even up to 100,000 miles. I've had lots of cloth-seat cars with well over 100,000 miles on them, and with upholstery that still looked like new.

How does the driver's seat feel when you sit in it? Is it firm and supportive, or does it feel sort of squished down in the middle? If all else is OK, a seat can be rebuilt to its original height and firmness, but figure at least $100 to do it at a good upholstery shop.

Even if these kinds of things aren't important to you, it's a good idea to take note of interior condition as an indicator of the care the car has received.

Now let's try out all the gadgets. Try all the power accessories through the full range of their operation. Take all the windows fully up and down, the seats all the way through all directions of travel, and don't forget mirrors, tilt-wheel, door locks, and the radio. Never operate a radio (or allow the seller to do so) while you're test-driving a car. Some sellers do it to distract your attention from things they'd just as soon forget. Now's the time to try it out.

Summary

Look over a prospective car very carefully to detect any sign of bodywork or repainting. Repainting is usually fairly easy to find if you know what to look for. Find evidence of masking by looking closely at edges of trim and under the edges of soft trim. Find evidence of spot-repairs and any bodywork by looking for paint surface irregularities. Irregularities are most easily spotted by looking at reflections in the surface of the paint. Any place that the paint gloss and surface looks different than on most of the rest of the car has most likely been repaired and repainted. Don't forget the engine compartment, cowl screens and door-edges for clues.

A car that's been hit doesn't necessarily need to be rejected. What you're looking for is an *indication* of repairs having been done, so that you or your expert friend can check further to find out the seriousness and full extent of the repair, and whether or not it was repaired right.

If you find a clue, and for example, you see some crinkles under a fender that look suspicious, take the car to a body shop and have an expert examine it.

You do not want to end up with a car that's had serious structural damage, or any damage at all that wasn't properly repaired! Visible rust or evidence of rust-repairs are both reasons to reject a car. Rust only keeps getting worse. Visible rust on an otherwise OK car is a safer bet than a freshly repainted car that show signs of rust-repairs. With a freshly repainted car, you have no way of knowing the extent of the rust. And remember: rust repairs are always temporary!

CHECK IT OUT
UNDER THE HOOD AND UNDER THE CAR

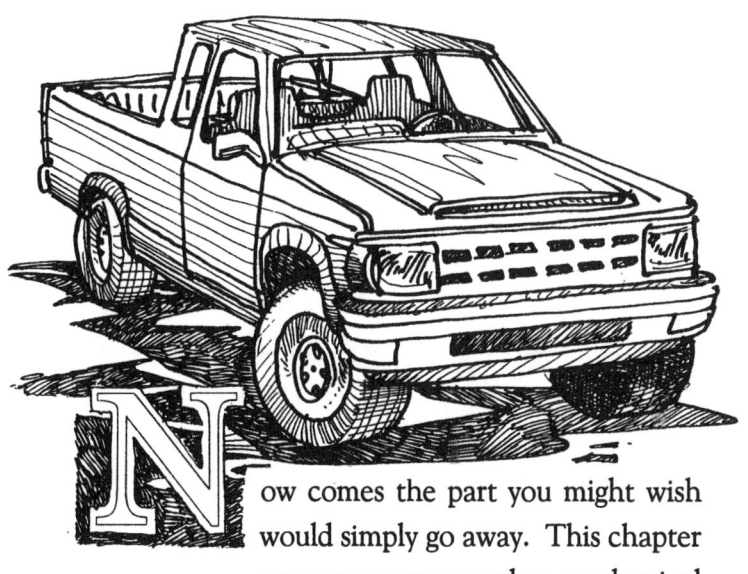

Now comes the part you might wish would simply go away. This chapter presents pretty complete mechanical checklist. Most people don't go to this much trouble inspecting a car, and you might not want to, either. But it won't hurt to read through the information just so you'll be familiar with what's here. That way, if you're looking over a car and something isn't right, you'll remember reading about it and can then check further. Also, don't forget the Pocket Checklist at the end of the book. It'll guide you through the following tests, and then if you need more info, each item is referenced back to the page where it appears in the book.

If you're looking at a car on a dealer's lot, this is a good time to remember that you should *ignore* everything that the salesman has to say. *He is not legally liable for anything he tells you,* so to listening to him just diverts your attention from the issue at hand: inspecting the car.

You're best off to assume that everything the salesman tells you is a lie, a diversion, or both. This might be unfair to the salesmen with integrity, but their numbers are small enough that we'll have to take that chance. Even if you're looking at a car offered by a private party, it's best to make your own evaluations and not let what the seller tells you influence your decision. The exception is if the seller has some documented evidence of work that was done on the car.

Use your own judgment or that of the knowledgeable friend you brought with you. (By the way, it's never a good idea to rely on the "expertise" of someone whose own car is always broken!)

Tires

So where do you begin? How about a walk-around inspection? You've already looked over the body (Chapter 14), but now pay particular attention to the tires. Their condition can speak volumes. Ideally, the tires should all be worn evenly and should reflect the mileage shown on the odometer. For example, if you're looking at a 20,000 mile car sporting brand-new tires, something is probably wrong. No car that you want to be the next owner of wears out a set of tires in 20,000 miles. File away discrepancies like this for later in your evaluation.

Most cars in normal use (assuming that the tires have been rotated as per manufacturer's recommendations) will get *at least* 35,000 miles out of a set of tires; some get 50,000 or more. Use these figures as a guide to determine whether or not the tires match the miles.

If the tires show any abnormal wear on one side or the other of the tread, especially the outside, suspect either very hard driving or an out-of-alignment front suspension. Another indication of front suspension problems is if the wear on one of the tires is noticeably different from the other. Don't just look at the front tires, either. It is common practice to put the best two on the front and the edgy ones back where they will be less likely to be examined.

Tires that are worn a lot more in the middle of the tread have been run with too much air-pressure. If the tread is OK in the middle but both edges are worn off, they've been run under-inflated. Irregular wear on the front tires, like a wavy wear-pattern or spots that are more worn that the rest of the tire indicate serious front-suspension problems or in some cases, a tire that's about to blow. Any car that has brand-new tires, especially if the mileage doesn't support this, should be carefully observed during the suspension-check part of the test drive (Chapter 16). The reason is that sellers will often put new tires on if the old ones revealed problems with the car.

Engine

If everything looks good so far, let's check the engine. Many dealers (and some individuals) start their cars every morning to warm them up so that they will crank over easily for customers. If you buy an already-warmed-up car, you might have a surprise in store for you the first time you try to start it cold.

Make sure you are starting a cold engine. *Before* getting in to start it, open the hood and carefully touch the radiator. It should be cold. If it is not, be aware of the possibility that the car had been warmed up earlier to disguise cold-starting problems. This is a distant possibility, but it is something to be aware of, especially if there doesn't appear to have been any reason for the car to be warmed up when you get there.

In many newer cars the radiator is nearly inaccessible; in this case, check for engine heat on any portion of the engine that's not too hot to touch.

Also, before starting the engine, let's check the cooling system, engine oil, and automatic transmission. The cooling system includes more parts than just the radiator, but the radiator is the easiest place to check the overall condition of the whole system. Only if the radiator is cool enough to remove the cap safely (like you can rest your hand comfortably on the radiator or engine), look in and see what the coolant looks like. It should be bright and clear, and the bright-greenish color of new antifreeze. If it looks even slightly black or brown, or the bottom of the radiator cap is covered with a greasy, dark film, *look out.* This is a strong indication of combustion products in the coolant. The only way combustion products can get into the coolant is with a blown head gasket, or a crack in the block or cylinder head. Yucky-looking coolant is a reason to disqualify a car.

Unfortunately, a cooling-system problem can be easily hidden from view by simply cleaning or replacing the radiator cap and wiping the grunge from the inside of the radiator filler neck (the short tube that connects the radiator cap to the radiator itself). If you have any reason to suspect that a problem exists, it would be wise to take the inspection one step further: stick your finger down into the radiator and take a sample from the inside of the radiator tank. Just reach in as far as you can, and rub your fingertip around wherever you can reach. Your finger should show only nice, clean coolant; no dark-colored, greasy stuff. There is no reason for a healthy engine to ever have any oily or sooty deposits in its cooling system. Unfortunately, many new cars have such a small filler-neck that a finger doesn't fit in very far. Just do your best!

Another place to look for cooling-system grunge is in the plastic radiator-overflow tank present on many cars. (This tank receives the excess coolant as it expands from being heated by the engine. Then as the engine cools, the coolant returns to the radiator, keeping the radiator full at all times.)

Incidentally, when checking the coolant level in a car not equipped with such a tank, the cold coolant level in the radiator is normally a couple inches below the top. This allows for the expansion of the coolant as the engine comes up to temperature.

Observe the areas around the radiator, particularly close to the filler, for any rusty-colored residue. This is often a telltale of a cooling system that has overheated, or a past or present leak in a hose or fitting. Any car that has ever been overheated should be rejected right away. One more time: *never, ever* open a radiator unless the engine is cool enough that you can comfortably lay your hand on it. Cooling systems are under pressure when hot, and can spray hot coolant all over you if you open the radiator cap.

If you are in a coastal area, check the core of the radiator, too. Salty air will rot the tiny fins of the radiator core, and the fins are absolutely necessary for the radiator to do its job. If you can reach it, lightly rub a finger over the radiator core and feel for a softness or mushiness of the cooling fins. (You might have to reach it from the engine side, through the cooling fan.) *Do this only with a cold engine, as the fan can start any time when the engine is at normal temperature.* I've seen radiators only a few years old with fins all but gone! If at all possible, check the front of the radiator. That's where the damage will occur first. A radiator with the fins gone or rotted cannot cool the engine properly. If you find a car with this condition, it would be wise to suspect that its engine has already been overheated. Pay special attention to the temperature gauge in your test-drive.

Engine Oil

Now pull out the engine-oil dipstick. The oil should be in the "safe" zone on the dipstick. This is usually pretty easy to see; there will be two lines or marks on the dipstick, and they designate the maximum and minimum oil levels. The oil should look like oil, not tar. Ideally, it should be fairly clean. (Clean engine oil looks like new vegetable oil. It will usually have a golden tint, about like clear honey.)

Absolutely clean indicates that it was just changed, which could either be a sign of good service or that somebody just did it to help the sale, because the old oil was really ugly and hadn't been changed in a long time. There's no way to tell, unless there are lube stickers on the car somewhere indicating that regular oil changes have been done. These stickers will be in any of several places: on the upper-left corner of the windshield (inside), on the back edge of the driver's door, on the underside of the hood, on the air-cleaner or other engine surface, or on the metal framework that supports the radiator.

When inspecting the oil on the dipstick, look for any indications of water. Water and oil don't mix, so if there is any moisture in the bottom of the engine where the oil lives, it will show as either tiny bubbles in the oil, or the oil itself will have a milky appearance. Either way, it's bad news. A healthy engine has no moisture in the oil.

Oil filters are usually visible from the engine compartment; check to see if it appears to have been recently changed. It will be a lot cleaner than surrounding engine parts if it has. An oil filter that's as covered with grime as the rest of the engine indicates the car has received little maintenance.

Automatic Transmission

Let's move on to the automatic transmission. Pull out the transmission dipstick and inspect the fluid. (On rear-wheel-drive cars, it will be located near the back of the engine compartment, and on front-wheel-drives, near the front of the engine compartment close to where the engine connects to the transmission.) The transmission fluid should be transparent and pink with no brown tinge or opaqueness. Sniffing the end of the dipstick should reveal a sweet odor. If the fluid has even the slightest hint of burnt smell, and/or the color is anything but transparent pink/red, the transmission is worn past the limits of any possible adjustments and is guaranteed to fail shortly. How do you identify "burnt" smell? You'll just know.

If your dream car proves to be a "10" in every respect except for a dubious transmission, buy it only if you can get a discount in the amount of a replacement transmission. And don't take the seller's word for how much that will be!

Back to the Engine

When you get in the car, turn on the ignition, and, again, *before* starting the engine, observe the gauges or warning lights. If there are no gauges for oil pressure, engine temperature or charging performance, there will be warning lights, (sometimes referred to as "idiot lights") and they should come on when the ignition is first switched on.

If any of the warning lights fail to light when the ignition is turned on, there is a problem. It could be any of several things: a burned-out bulb (not likely), a problem in the system that the light is a warning for, or the light could have been disconnected in an attempt to hide such a problem.

Since almost nobody checks these lights before starting the engine, it is easy to disable the oil-pressure light, for example, to disguise the fact that the oil pressure is so low that the light won't go off when the engine is started. (If I sound particularly distrustful, let me assure you that all of the tricks outlined in this book are in common use in the car business. And not just by little, low-budget dealers, either.)

Start the engine. A properly-tuned engine in good condition will start instantly. If you have to crank the engine for even ten seconds or longer, there's something wrong. It could be as simple as a tuneup, but chances are good that if the engine does not start quickly, the rest of these tests will disqualify it.

The instant the engine starts, go back to those warning lights. If everything is operating normally, the warning lights will go out as soon as the engine comes to life. The oil-pressure light should go out as soon as the engine is cranked over. If the oil-pressure light comes on occasionally at idle after getting the engine fully warmed up, you have an indication of a tired engine.

This light should never come on, not even flicker, while the engine is running. The only exception is in a thoroughly warmed-up engine at idle with the air-conditioning turned on, causing the engine idle-speed to be very low. This is still an indication of a problem, but it could be in the device that speeds up the idle when the air-conditioning compressor comes on rather than excessively low oil pressure. If you do experience an occasional flickering of the oil light under these circumstances, turn off the air. If the resulting increase in engine speed doesn't turn off the light, go look at another car.

If the car has a real oil-pressure gauge instead of an idiot light, the oil-pressure gauge will immediately read at the high end of its scale when the engine comes to life (assuming that the engine is cold). The ammeter will go to full charge and then in a few moments start to come back closer to the middle. A voltmeter will go up toward the high end of its scale (somewhere around fourteen or fifteen volts depending of the individual gauge and the car).

The charge-indicator light might come on occasionally at idle, especially with a heavy load on the electrical system. For example, with headlights, wipers, and the heater all going, it would be normal on some cars for the charge light to come on occasionally at a low idle. It should go off as soon as the engine speed is increased.

The temperature gauge shouldn't do much of anything. The engine-temperature warning light comes on only when the temperature has risen to a dangerous level, well above the normal range of operation. Some temperature warning lights come on at such a high temperature that if you can't shut off the engine instantly, there will be some damage. In other instances, like when the overheating is caused by a coolant leak, the light might not come on at all. This is because the little sensors in the cooling system are designed to detect high temperatures when immersed in the liquid coolant. Some of them will not respond in an environment of air, as when the coolant has all leaked out.

Gauges have it all over warning lights. Gauges warn you of *impending* problems; the lights generally don't come on until the problems are extreme.

Once I was driving a nearly-new Buick Riviera at freeway speed, and the "hot" light came on. Before I could stop the car, the engine was toast. Had this car been equipped with gauges, I would have been warned of the problem in advance by seeing the temperature start to climb above its normal operating range.

If the car you're examining has gauges, check them with the engine running *and* again with it turned off. Make sure that the oil-pressure and engine-temperature gauges read zero or are at the bottom of their ranges of operation with the engine off. If there is an ammeter (it would read zero in the middle, "plus" or "charge" on the right side of the scale, and "minus" or "discharge" on the left), it should be centered on zero with the engine off. If there is a volt meter (more common on newer cars), it should read zero, again, with the engine off.

Why check the gauges with the engine off? We're checking for more dirty little tricks! Again, most people never look at the gauges before starting the engine, making possible little tricks like this: I once bought a really nice Subaru wagon at a dealer auction. Of course, I checked the oil-pressure gauge while driving the car on the test track. It looked great. I got the car home before noticing that the oil pressure read normal pressure whether the engine was running or not! Someone had taken the cover off the instrument panel and stuffed a carefully-trimmed wedge from a paper match under the needle on the gauge so that it stayed at a normal-pressure reading. He assumed, correctly, that a buyer would not bother to observe the oil-pressure gauge unless the engine was running.

As it turned out, the Subaru needed only an inexpensive oil pressure sending unit; the engine was fine. But someone had gone to the trouble to do the dirty deed.

As the engine warms up, the oil pressure will drop slightly, the temperature gauge will start to climb to the middle of its "normal" range, and a voltmeter reading will taper off somewhat. A thorough test-drive will now allow the gauges to give you a lot of valuable information about the condition of the engine.

A fully warmed-up (normal operating-temperature) engine should still show normal-range oil pressure. A reading of less than twenty pounds (near the bottom of a numberless gauge) at idle is suspect. If the oil pressure drops significantly as the engine warms up, the cause is most likely a very worn engine that's not going to go much farther without major problems.

If this low oil-pressure phenomenon shows up in a fairly low-mileage car, it could be simply a faulty sending unit, or it could be wear--particularly if the car had been abused and rarely serviced. In any event, low or erratic oil pressure is a good reason to reject the car.

The temperature should remain constant even during hill climbing and stop-and-go driving. Many temperature-related problems can be traced to a faulty thermostat or cooling-fan switch. If the temperature never comes up to normal, the cause is most likely a stuck-open thermostat. Or a missing thermostat. The cheapest fix for a bad thermostat is to remove it. The only problem is that the engine will never come up to normal operating temperature, and the temperature will not be stabilized under varying loads. A clear symptom of this "fix" is a heater which will not produce warm air.

A stuck-shut thermostat will cause the engine to overheat. It is unlikely that anyone will offer a car in this condition for sale, because a stuck-shut thermostat will cause the engine to overheat almost immediately. As soon as the engine is started, the temperature will just start climbing and climb until the coolant boils.

If the engine seems to heat up too easily, like when climbing steep, long hills or idling in traffic, the problem is elsewhere and this is reason enough to reject the car.

Another common cause for late-model cars to heat up while idling or poking along in traffic is the electric cooling fan not coming on when it should. This can be the result of a bad temperature switch in the radiator, a faulty fan motor, or maybe even a repairman having inadvertently unplugged the connection while performing a non-related repair or service.

After the engine is fully warmed, and with the car parked, rev it up a few times and observe the exhaust. This is best accomplished with someone else doing the revving so that you can be behind the car observing the exhaust. (By "revving," we mean to punch the gas pedal a few times enough to really speed up the engine, but *not to excess*.) There should be absolutely no smoke whatsoever.

Checking the condition of the hoses and belts can tell what kind of maintenance the car has been receiving. No conscientious car owner will allow belts to get old enough to start fraying or cracking. Radiator and heater hoses should be supple and free of cracks and bulges.

If the car you are interested in is more than four years old, the belts and hoses should have been replaced by now. Replacement hoses can generally be spotted by new hose clamps which don't match the originals, and the hoses will look fresher than the surrounding parts.

Air cleaners can give clues about engine condition and previous maintenance. It the engine has a carburetor, remove the top of the air cleaner. The paper filter should be reasonably clean and in good condition. The inside of the air cleaner housing itself should be clean, too. If there is any oil in the bottom of the air cleaner, this engine either has worn piston rings or there are some problems with the anti-pollution system. If the car you're looking over has fuel-injection, the air-cleaner element will be under a cover with easy-to-remove clips. Just lift up the clips and you can raise the cover to inspect the paper element.

CV Joints

On front-wheel-drive autos and on the small four-wheel-drive vehicles, the drive shafts which connect the transaxle and differential to the wheels have constant-velocity universal joints on each end. These CV joints (as they are commonly called) are extremely expensive and prone to early failure when not maintained properly.

The most common reason for premature failure is a break in the protective rubber boot which covers the joint. The grease runs out; water, abrasive dirt, snow and slush get in; and the precision-machined internal parts fail quickly. Boots are often damaged by something as simple as stones kicked up from the road by the wheels, so periodic inspection is an essential part of vehicle maintenance.

Once you get into your test-drive (Chapter 16), there are some simple tests which will make a defective CV joint speak to you.

Look Underneath!

A hoist is a valuable aid in checking out a car. Of course, the problem is finding a mechanic with a hoist. Used to be, all service stations had hoists. Now they have mini-marts instead.

From underneath, you will be able to see symptoms of any problems that the usual steam-cleaning job will erase from view if your inspections are limited to under-hood.

If you do get your prospective auto up on a hoist, inspect the bottom of the engine for evidence of oil leaking from the front seal. A front seal leak would show up in the form of a buildup of oily sludge on the bottom of the oil pan, especially near the front, and on surrounding components. In a severe case of any kind of an oil leak, there might even be shiny metal, kept clean by the continuous flow of oil.

Other specific areas to check for leaks are the fuel and oil pumps, transmission and torque-converter, power steering pump and hoses, transmission cooler plumbing, and the seals on tie-rod ends and other steering and suspension parts. Check also for leaking shock absorbers and evidence of brake cylinder/caliper leaks.

OK, where *are* all these things and how do you find them? Well, I'm assuming that you have the car on a hoist at this point, and most hoists are in garages and come with mechanics! And this is also why you brought along your knowledgeable friend.

I'm hoping that you aren't allowing yourself to feel lost with all this techno-stuff. I realize that this is new information to most people (not just women), and am hoping that you take in as much of this information as you're comfortable with and leave the rest for either later (when it's more specific to your needs), or pass it on to whomever will be helping you evaluate a car.

If you are doing this all by yourself, I recommend that you just do the best you can looking for leaks. It's normal for the bottom of a car to be messy and dirty, but it's not normal for there to be any drips of anything! Actively leaking fluids coming from anywhere are signs of problems that need to be addressed (or avoided). Unusually thick buildups of greasy grunge are signs of oil or grease leaks, too.

If you see any evidence of leaks anywhere, ask your mechanic to explain their source and implications for future problems.

One more check your mechanic can make while the car is in the air is for front-suspension and ball-joint wear. This is especially important on a car with over about fifty-thousand miles on it. Front suspension wear is directly proportional to the kinds of roads the car has been driven on for most of its life. Some fifty-thousand mile cars will have suspension components worn to the point where a proper front-end alignment is no longer possible, and others will be in near-perfect condition. Front end repairs are expensive. An overhaul can cost $400-800, depending on the car.

If you care to go so far as to remove a front wheel, you can inspect the condition of the brake rotors and pads. Any attention needed in these areas can be negotiated in the price of the car.

When I ask you to do things like "check the brake rotors and pads," I'm assuming one of two things: you either know what these things are already, or you've got somebody with you who can help. If you have a helper, get that person to talk you through the inspections so you'll know what to look for next time! And having one of those auto-parts-store manuals for your car is a big help, too. Then you can look up the part in question and it will be clearly identified for you. I highly recommend you get one!

If there's just no practical way you can look under the car, at least check the pavement under the car after it's moved from where it was parked. If there are any fresh-looking spots that indicate leaks, you need to follow up on these. Also, even if you can't get the car up in the air, if it's a front-wheel drive, peek underneath (or have your car-person friend do it) and do a visual check of the CV-joint boots. These are a common problem, and they're in the neighborhood of $100 each to replace, and that's if there's no internal damage. The inner ones can usually be seen from under the hood, but the outers must be checked by looking under the car itself.

One last thing before the test drive is to check the shocks. With your knee on the bumper, put your weight on the car enough to make it bounce up and down a couple of times. When you stop and get away from the car, it should come back to its original position with no more than one more bounce, and that one should be barely discernable. You can do this most easily by doing each corner of the car, but then also do it from the middle of each bumper. The car should go up and down evenly; it should not move farther on one side than the other. Any excessive or uneven bounce indicates worn or leaking shock absorbers. Either way, the only cure is replacement. Most tire shops listed in the Yellow Pages also install shocks, and can give you a quotation on the particular car you're looking at.

OK, how does the condition of this car compare to the mileage on the odometer? Does the mileage seem reasonable? Here are some considerations on odometer readings.

Don't let an odometer sell you the car. Don't even trust the odometer in the first place! Although recent laws have deterred most shaky dealers from "spinning speedos," it hasn't stopped them all. And the worst culprits are actually not the dealers, but the private parties from whom the dealers get the cars as trade-ins. Here's how that works.

There are a lot of people who feel that since most dealers are crooks anyway, what's the harm in beating them at their own game by selling or trading in a car with an "adjusted" odometer reading? Also, up until a few years ago, most cars had odometers which only read up to 99,999 miles. Many times cars with 30,000 or 40,000 miles on the odometer are traded in as showing "true mileage" when in fact the meter has already rolled over once.

A dealer taking in a car like this might never suspect that the car has an extra 100,000 miles on it, but more than likely, he *will* suspect it but not acknowledge it. He can resell the car to someone and not have to worry about the misrepresentation as long as he has a signed mileage document from the person who traded in the car.

I've seen many cars at the auctions showing 20,000, 30,000, or 40,000 miles and looking for all the world like this was the true mileage, only to hear them announced by the auctioneer as "miles over" (the odometer had gone past 100,000 miles and started over). Sometimes, finding out the truth can take very careful examination.

If the procedures outlined in this chapter still leave you wondering if the speedo is accurate, consult your competent mechanic for a diagnosis. Sometimes the only way to tell is by carefully listening to the engine. A trained ear can usually hear the difference. (See Chapter 14 for more specifics.)

Summary

An automobile is a complex machine, and there are lots of possibilities for mechanical problems. A careful inspection will find not only existing problems, but potential future problems, as well.

Just driving a car around the block isn't a valid check of all its various systems and components. Generally, the older the car and the more miles it shows on the odometer, the more thorough of an inspection is required. But that *is* a generalization! A one-year-old car with only 17,000 miles on it is not necessarily without serious problems. The inspections outlined in this chapter are suggested for any car that you're unfamiliar with. The only time I'd recommend a less thorough inspection is if you're buying a car you're familiar with from someone you know (and trust).

Take the Pocket Check-List with you when you go to look at a car. It will give you a guide to all the things to look at, along with page-references back to the book if you need more information.

THE TEST DRIVE

This is the fun part. You've looked the car over and you're satisfied that it's at least good enough to try a test drive. All the outside stuff and the cosmetics checked out OK. If you've never driven a sample of this particular make and model, you might even want to drive it before you spend a lot of time checking the details. Why waste your time (and the seller's) if you don't care for the way the car feels when you drive it?

If after driving the car you're still interested, a more careful inspection might then be in order, depending on how carefully you examined it beforehand.

Tell the seller that you want to do a *real* test drive, not just a drive around the block. You want to take the car out on the highway, up and down some hills, let it poke along in traffic, and then you want to find a big parking lot to check out the CV joints (if it's got front-wheel- or four-wheel-drive).

Then *take* a real test drive.

Observe how the car behaves before the engine is fully warmed up. It should accelerate smoothly from a stop. If it has a standard shift, the clutch should engage smoothly. (More on the clutch later.)

If the car accelerates roughly when cold, but seems to smooth out after the car is warmed up to normal operating temperature, there is possibly a problem in the cold-running circuits of the carburetor or fuel-injection.

If the cold engine persists in running roughly at any low-power throttle setting, but smooths out when you step on the gas a little harder, the problem is probably in the carburetor itself, assuming the car has a carburetor. It needs to be disassembled and cleaned. With electronic fuel-injection, it's time for a diagnostic checkup (expensive).

"It Just Needs Sparkplugs."

A lot of sellers, particularly private-party sellers, will put a car up for sale when it's running poorly. They'll tell you that it just needs sparkplugs, or maybe a minor tuneup, and that they just haven't had the time to deal with it. *Don't believe it!* What they're actually telling you is that the reason they're selling the thing is because they've tried every way they could think of to get the darned thing to run right and they're exasperated with it! You can safely assume that any seller will do what is practical to get a car running its best when trying to sell it. Few people will try to sell a car that's running badly if they *really believe* it would only take sparkplugs to fix it.

The Freeway Test

Take it out on the freeway. Get the car up to at least the speed you normally drive; higher would be better. If the car has gauges for oil-pressure and engine-temperature, this is a good time to watch them occasionally. The oil-pressure gauge should be at least in the middle of its range; a little toward the high end is better. If it doesn't come up to the middle, or "normal" range, suspect a very tired engine. The engine-temperature gauge should remain in its "normal" range under any driving condition. There is an engine problem if the temperature gauge goes up even to the high end of the "normal" range. If you see this happening, after your test-drive, pay particular atention to the cooling-system checks mentioned in the previous chapter. Especially if you now suspect a cooling problem, make sure your drive includes some slow speeds, too, as in a good traffic jam, watch the temperature gauge.

OK, back to the business of driving. Maintain speed for a while and pay attention to vibrations. Does the steering wheel shake a little? Any shake in the wheel indicates a problem. It could be something as simple as a slightly out-of-balance tire, but it could as well be something more serious. If everything else is OK, ask the seller to have the wheels balanced or to guarantee that he will take care of any necessary repairs beyond a wheel balance.

If the road is level, hold the wheel very lightly and watch for any tendency to pull to one side or the other. If the road is crowned off to the right, as many are, there will be a slight tendency for the car to favor the right side of the road. This is normal, particularly with rack and pinion steering.

If you get a chance to drive the car on a road that's crowned to the left, however, the car should then exhibit an equal tendency to pull to the left.

Brakes

Find a road with little or no traffic to test the brakes. At thirty or forty miles per hour, when you can look in your mirror and see no vehicles close behind you, warn your passenger(s) of your intentions, then press on the brake pedal hard enough to make a serious stop, but not hard enough to skid the tires. This test works best going down a fairly steep hill.

No amount of braking should lock up any one wheel. If a wheel does lock up (indicated by one tire screeching on the pavement), suspect a leaky wheel cylinder, defective caliper, or a leaky bearing seal that's allowing grease to get on the linings or pads. (This is a very unsafe condition, as the distance required to stop with a locked-up wheel is increased dramatically.)

On braking, there must be no pull to either side; the car should stop perfectly straight. You should feel no vibration in the brake pedal. A hard, constant brake application at thirty to forty miles per hour will demonstrate warped brake rotors with a firm pulsation you can feel in the brake pedal. Depending on how bad the rotors are, the pulsation may continue until the car comes to a stop. Warped brake rotors are a result of overheating the brakes, which can be done in a number of ways. The most common is "riding the brakes."

If you discover warped brake rotors on your prospective purchase, have the seller agree to repair the problem. If the rotors are still repairable, the cost to do the front brakes would be in the neighborhood of $100-$150. If the rotors need to be replaced, you're looking at a sizeable chunk of money. If he will agree, get him to pay to have the job done at the shop of your choice. And always get promises in writing. *Remember, if the seller is a dealer, he is not legally liable for any verbal agreements.*

Steering

For a test of the power steering and related systems, try this: With the car parked and the engine at idle, turn the steering wheel a full turn to one side and then to the other. The wheel should turn smoothly with no jumping or intermittent hesitations. If you feel a kind of intermittent resistance to your turning effort, make sure that the air-conditioning is off (to insure a normal idle speed). If that doesn't smooth it out, you are probably dealing with a fairly tired car, or at least one with some tired front suspension and/or steering components, and a more careful checkup in this area is in order.

Transmissions and Clutches

Now let's check the automatic transmission. From a full stop, accelerate at moderate throttle to about forty-five miles per hour while paying close attention to shifting. The shifts should be smooth, yet positive. You should not hear the engine revving even slightly as a shift occurs, and there should be no sign of "clunking" into gear on either up- or down-shifts.

If the speeds at which the automatic transmission shifts gears--or anything else about it-- seems unusual to you, consult your mechanic for an opinion.

The Clutch

You're looking at a five-speed? First, see how the clutch works.

Before you take off, check the free play of the clutch pedal. You should be able to press down lightly with your fingertips on the clutch pedal and feel (depending on make and model) from a half-inch to a little over an inch of "play" before the pedal comes in contact with the clutch mechanism. It's hard to describe in words, but you'll know what it is when you feel it. For the first inch or so, the pedal goes down fingertip easy, and then it hits a spot where it takes your foot to push it down any farther.

The reason for this check is to determine whether or not the clutch is in proper adjustment. The clutch adjustment is done at the pedal; if it is correctly adjusted, there will be the proper amount of free play. If there is no free play, or if the pedal moves several inches before engaging the clutch, it is out of adjustment. It's difficult to determine the condition of the clutch itself when it's out of adjustment.

A poorly-adjusted clutch pedal is highly suspect in a car for sale. It means either the car has been poorly taken care of, or that the pedal has been deliberately maladjusted to disguise a worn-out clutch.

When you let out the clutch, it must engage smoothly and positively. The clutch should start to engage when it is about half way up from the floor. Closer to the floor is OK, but much more than half way up speaks of a worn clutch which may need replacement soon. Any shuddering or vibration felt upon clutch engagement means replacement is on the near horizon, and that the entire clutch assembly will need replacement, not just the friction disc.

When cruising along in fourth gear at about twenty-five or thirty miles per hour on level ground and at a light throttle, push the clutch in very lightly (just far in enough to barely release) for just a brief moment and then let it right back out. It should engage firmly and with no perceptible increase in engine speed. If the re-engagement results in some engine speed-up and/or feels at all mushy, the clutch might well be worn out. If you have any doubts about the results of this test, make a note of it on the checklist for your mechanic. (A clutch can be expected to last from 40,000 to over 100,000 miles in normal use, depending on the driving conditions.

Daily driving in the San Francisco hills will wear out a clutch much faster than freeway commuting, even with a careful driver.)

Manual Transmission

The weakest parts in most manual transmissions are the synchronizers, or "synchros." The job of the synchros is to instantly adjust the speeds of the gears as you shift, enabling the individual gears to mesh without grinding. If a transmission has been abused by hard shifting, the synchros wear out prematurely, making it difficult to shift without grinding the gears. The best way to check for worn synchros is to do exactly what you're not supposed to do: shift fast and hard.

Just this one time, pretend you are on a race track. Accelerate to get to sixty miles per hour as if your life depends on it. Shift quickly and firmly. The shifts should be smooth and quiet. Any grinding noise as you shift into the next gear means shot synchros, and shot synchros only get worse. If you can make them misbehave with this test, it won't be too long before you notice the grinding during normal shifting.

One more test: when you get into top gear, shift back down, quickly and firmly, through each gear as you bring the car back to a stop. Again, the shifts should be smooth and quiet. You will likely feel some resistance in the shift lever on down shifting, particularly if done at higher than normal speeds. Just this once it's OK. Shifts should, at all times, be smooth and quiet.

I really take it easy on cars, and I've bought a few cars with bad synchros just because I resist "speed-shifting." But I have learned to shift up and down through all the gears, hard and fast, on a test drive. Any gear-crunching on a hard shift means that at least one previous owner made a habit of that kind of shifting, and unless you're prepared to replace the transmission, you don't want the car.

A note on down-shifting: many people seem to think that they should shift down through each gear every time they come to a stop. Continual down-shifting is the kiss of death to transmission synchros. Generally, the only time it's necessary to down-shift is when approaching a long downhill stretch where you will need compression (the resistance, or slowing-effect, provided by the engine) to avoid riding the brakes. In average driving situations, the proper way to come to a normal stop is to anticipate the stop early, and take your foot off the gas to allow the car to decelerate naturally so that a light braking will bring you to a stop.

Brakes last a long time and are fairly inexpensive to reline. Transmissions are real spendy to fix. To shift down through each gear every time you come to a stop is putting a lot of unnecessary wear on your transmission.

C-V Joints

Find a place to make some sharp, slow-speed turns. Parking lots work fine for this. Turn the wheel all the way to one side, and in a low gear at very low speed, step on the gas fairly hard for a moment, and listen. Now turn to the opposite side and repeat the operation. What you're supposed to hear is nothing.

If you hear a "click-click-click" noise, or something similar, one of the CV joints is going out on the side to which you were turning. This test will identify defective CV joints on either end of a four-wheel-drive.

Another test for finding defective CV joints on both ends of most 4x4s, is a hard stop. This is best done on a short, steep hill to go down, where you will have more time to listen for noises. Get the car going twenty miles per hour or so, and then brake fairly hard; just not quite hard enough to stop the car before you get to the bottom of the hill. The same "click-click-click" noise will tell you of a defective CV joint.

Unless a boot has been broken or torn, CV joints on most cars don't usually cause before seventy or eighty thousand miles. And on a well-maintained car that's seen careful use, they can last twice that long. But it's important to find the defective ones in your prospective purchase, because the repairs are spendy. In some cars, the entire shaft assembly with both joints must be replaced, and they cost in the $300-500 range. Each.

Summary

The road-test can be done before or after your careful mechanical and body check. The advantage of doing at least a cursory check before the road test is that any possible problems you find beforehand can be verified in the road test.

Conversely, make a note of any problems you discover in your road test that can later be verified in a mechanical or body inspection. The best procedure is to combine all of your evaluation efforts so that they'll support each other.

Pay attention to your findings, and ignore the stories from the seller. A dealer will try to keep your focus off of the car with general conversation about anything but the car. A private-party seller will have a ready excuse for every problem you discover. Trust your evaluation, and that of the expert you bring with you!

Taking a few extra minutes to do a thorough examination of a prospective purchase can save a lot of frustration and expense down the road.

All this testing may have you thinking that I feel most used cars are lemons. Not at all! Not all used cars are defective! All used cars have flaws. Many new cars have flaws. And the job of disguising defective vehicles has become an art-form, so you just need to be careful. After all, you're going to be living with this purchase for a while, and it isn't *that* difficult to check it out completely.

It's important to know *enough* about cars and how to check them out that you'll know when someone is trying to sell you a bill of goods.

It isn't necessary to be mechanically inclined to have a basic understanding of how cars work, either. Having that understanding will serve you well, not only in getting a fair deal in buying a car and keeping it running, but also in having some kind of idea of what's happening when a problem does come up. That knowledge can not only save you tow bills, long walks, and unnecessary repairs, it can give you some really comfortable peace of mind.

WHAT TO DO WHEN IT BREAKS

Are you aware that many women actually believe that there's some mysterious phenomenon about their gender that precludes their being able to understand anything mechanical?

I get this again and again, and it's always a mystery. A friend tells me she had a problem with her car, and how much she paid to have it fixed. When I timidly suggest that it should have cost about half of what she paid, she says that she always takes her car to the same guy, and she trusts him. I've even been told that I should butt out; that this guy always manages to get the car running again, and it's worth whatever it costs.

Well, it's good to feel you can trust somebody, but there are those who will take advantage of *anybody* when they think it's going to be easy. And I guess it's also nice to be able to afford "whatever it costs." However, it's not easy to take advantage of somebody who is well-informed!

You don't need to be a mechanic to be able to make some intelligent decisions about car repairs. All it takes is common sense, and that's one of the survival skills that almost all women are blessed with. Sure, some basic understanding of the most fundamental functions of your car are certainly an asset, but even that isn't absolutely necessary.

If you resist getting involved, then you need a car-savvy friend you can trust. And that person needs to be somebody other than your mechanic! The only car-help you'll ever need from that friend is an occasional look or listen to your car when it's misbehaving, and enough of a diagnosis that you'll know if your mechanic is trying to pad the bill or sell you something you don't need.

It's kind of like going to a general practitioner with a medical problem. He checks out the basics, tells you what's wrong, and can then sends you to the specialist who knows exactly how to deal with the problem. With your car, maybe your friend can even fix it right then and there with just a knowing twist of a screwdriver. And if you're paying attention, you can do it yourself if it ever happens again!

There's nothing mysterious about how cars work, and fixing them isn't necessarily a "guy thing." Sure, you don't see a whole lot of women working as mechanics, but there are some who do, and they're every bit as competent as the men they work alongside of. I believe the fact that most mechanics are men has a less to do with what most women are *able* to do than with what they would *rather* do.

There are several ways you can become car-savvy with a minimum of effort. One is to buy a shop manual on your specific car and just look through it. Find anything that seems to be of interest at the moment and read about it. Go out and compare what you've read to what it really looks like on your own car, then the next time you need a repair done, see if you can locate the problem-part in your manual and figure out what it will take to fix it. You don't need to fix it yourself, just get an idea of what it will take, and then when you talk to your mechanic you'll be able to tell right away if he's being straight with you about the repair. Wouldn't that feel better than having to accept whatever he tells you because you don't have a clue as to what he's talking about?

For example, say you hear this scraping noise when you step on the brakes. You go to your book and by looking at the pictures of your front disc brakes and then checking the troubleshooting section on disc brakes, you can easily tell that your brake pads are so badly worn that they have started to scrape the rotors. Then you look at the step-by-step pictures of how to replace a rotor, and it becomes clear to you that this isn't much of a job. Now you can even call a brake shop and get a phone quote for replacing your brake pads and rotors before you take the car to your regular mechanic. When your man gives you his price, you'll know exactly how fair he's being with you.

Too much trouble? Well, it might take you an extra half-hour to do what I just described, but how about if what you learn in that time saves you a hundred dollars? Add the savings to the confidence you'll build by gradually learning the basics about how your car works, and it comes out to a pretty good deal!

Most shop manuals, even the inexpensive ones available through most auto-parts stores, have good troubleshooting sections. These list all sorts of symptoms, and then give you the probable causes. From there, the book will show how to correct the problem. Familiarizing yourself with the basics can save you a lot of repair-dollars over the years. Chances are excellent that you'll save many times the cost of the book on your next repair. You might even find it so interesting that you'll read the whole book!

Big Noise; Small Problem

Lots of seemingly major malfunctions are just little glitches that happen to make a lot of noise. The trick is to get familiar with your car *and its normal sounds*. Then when you hear something that is out of the ordinary, have it looked at immediately! Never ignore an unusual noise coming from your car! Those noises are your car asking for needed attention.

Important: *More often than not, immediate attention to a strange noise will allow you to quickly and cheaply repair a problem that will turn into a major bummer if ignored.*

Roadside Emergencies

This book takes a unique approach to dealing with on-the-road mechanical problems. Rather than present you with a long table of things that can happen, symptoms to look for, probable causes and the appropriate fix for each, you will learn how to avoid the break-down in the first place. It's a little like taking good care of your body and staying in good health, instead of carrying an enormous first-aid kit and a list of medical specialists and hospital phone numbers with you at all times.

For example, what makes more sense; to keep a gas can in your trunk for when you run out of gas, or to watch your gas gauge and fill the tank when you should? Well, that's pretty obvious, but so are almost all of the preventive maintenance items that will keep your car from coming unglued at inopportune moments.

Some people choose to keep duct-tape in the trunk for emergency repairs of broken radiator hoses. I choose to keep good radiator hoses on my car so I don't have to worry about them. I have never known a hose to fail for any other reason than simple old age deterioration. The same thing applies to most maintenance items.

The truth is that you could keep your whole trunk full of tools and "emergency supplies" and *still* not have what it takes for a fix. And that's assuming that you're a mechanic!

Another truth is that well-maintained cars rarely break.

About the only "roadside repair" that can happen to the best maintained car in the world, is a flat tire. All it takes is running over a nail or some other sharp debris on the road. I recommend that you familiarize yourself with the jack in your car, and how to use it, in the safety and convenience of your driveway or garage. Remove the jack, read the instruction placard that shows exactly where you are to place the jack against the frame of the car, and then actually do it. You don't have to take the car off the ground or actually remove a wheel, but if you find the jacking points on your car and go through the motions one time in good light and on level, dry ground, it will be much easier if you ever need to do it out on the road. Dealing with a flat on a dark, rainy night can be a lot less unpleasant if you know exactly what you're doing! (Don't forget to firmly set the parking brake before jacking up your car!)

Major Repairs

    An automobile is an incredibly complex machine. It's actually a combination of many complex individual machines, each of which must perform perfectly all the time, under all conditions, with anyone at all operating the controls. It is not surprising then, especially considering the abuse that many cars must endure, that some parts of these wonderful machines occasionally malfunction.
    Most machinery, whether it's in a big factory or in your kitchen at home, comes with very complete operating instructions. Even your food-processor and sewing machine is supplied with instructions and many cautions, reminding you of what can go wrong if the rules aren't strictly adhered to.

All cars come with an owner's manual. (That's the book that lives in most people's glove box and never gets looked at.) The instructions in these manuals are very basic and assumes that everything is functioning normally. Most of these books, especially the ones that come with domestic cars, will just refer you to your dealer in the even anything goes wrong.

Here's one of the most complex pieces of machinery available to the general public, and it has to be designed to be foolproof. It has to do its thing exactly the same way for an experienced, careful operator as for someone who has never driven a car before. It has to work perfectly for drivers who have not the foggiest notion of what makes it all happen. And as our cars grow ever more complicated, more and more devices need to be engineered and installed so that the whole package will *still* be fool-proof.

The folks who trade in their cars for new ones every year or two probably never have to deal with a major repair. Were they to do an objective analysis of the costs of this luxury, they would no doubt be astonished. For example, you could do a couple of major engine overhauls for less than the cost of the *first-year depreciation* on most new cars.

You, on the other hand, haven't allowed yourself to be lured into this kind of extravagance! You decided long ago to get your money's worth out of your automobile, right? And you may get through your entire life without having to face the ultimate repair job: an engine replacement. But then, maybe not. What do you do when your trusted diagnostician says that you need a new engine? The first thing almost everyone does is to throw up their hands and think about buying another car. But with a little shopping around, fixing the one you've got can be a whole lot more cost-effective. So where do you go from there? Start pricing overhauled engines? Some people even go to their new-car dealer and price a brand new engine. Neither of these is the preferred alternative.

Let's see how your car came to need a new engine in the first place.

The car has likely been driven well over a hundred thousand miles, and the engine is just plain worn out. Maybe the car didn't receive all the oil-changes and other TLC it was supposed to for the last few years.

There are hundreds of wearing parts in your engine. And when they are almost all worn to the same degree, it makes no sense to do a band-aid repair, fixing just the worst-worn parts.

The Band-Aid Repair

There are lots of repair-shop owners/managers who will gladly take in your car when you complain of some specific problem, for example, excessive oil consumption. They'll tell you that they can just "put in a new set of rings" and you will get another fifty-thousand miles out of the old engine. Then, as soon as your car is in his shop with its engine mostly disassembled, you will, quite predictably, get "the phone call." The garagekeeper will explain to you that, upon inspecting the innards of your engine, he found that the engine really does need a complete overhaul. He is sorry to have to tell you, of course, and he WOULD, as he promised you to get your car in his shop, do just the rings, but he would not be able to guarantee his work.

This is one of the oldest sales gimmicks in the repair business. First, you are told that you don't need the expensive repair that someone else said you needed. *That gets your attention right away.* Then you get a promise of how the band-aid repair will save you a bunch of money. Now you're hooked. You turn over the keys, and you have become another sucker.

You will get the infamous phone call, and the price of a "proper" repair job will probably end up costing you more than the original quotation for an overhaul. The mechanic will cover himself by explaining to you that he will honor his original repair estimate, but he will also plant the seeds of doubt in your mind by telling you that he certainly couldn't guarantee his work if *you chose not to do the job right.*

He has effectively washed his hands of the whole affair, and it has suddenly become your problem. He also has your car disassembled in his shop. You will pay his price, the price he knew in the beginning he would get.

Almost any time a mechanic tells you that he can do a fairly major repair on a tired, high-mile engine in order to save you the cost of a complete overhaul, you are probably being set up to pay the price of a complete overhaul, and then some.

The irony of the whole thing is that most repair shops are not equipped to do overhauls properly anyway, so even after you end up paying the big bucks to get your car back, it still won't be right. In all my years in the car business, I have dealt with a large number of "overhauled" engines. I HAVE NEVER SEEN AN OVERHAULED ENGINE WHICH I WOULD HAVE WANTED IN MY OWN CAR.

The Overhauled Engine

The words "overhaul" and "rebuilt" mean different things to different people. To some less-than-reputable mechanics, a reasonably quiet engine or transmission with a good steam-cleaning and a fresh coat of paint qualifies as rebuilt.

Most reputable shops do not do their own overhauls. They buy "exchange overhaul" engine blocks from a large rebuild shop that does nothing but rebuild engines. They install one of these engine blocks in your car, and your old block then goes back to the rebuild shop as a "core" for another rebuild.

Rebuild shops, as every other business, come with varying degrees of integrity. Here's an example of what you might buy from even one of the better rebuild shops.

OK, this gets a little bit technical, but try it on anyway. Every part in an engine has a dimensional tolerance. (Dimensional tolerances are the parameters set for gauging worn parts. If wear exceeds dimensional tolerances, or size limit, the parts in question must be replaced.) If a main bearing journal, for example, is supposed to be 3" in diameter, but is allowed a wear tolerance of .003" before a replacement is called for, the shop may with a clear conscience, re-use a crankshaft that measures .00299" undersize. It is, as they say, "within tolerance."

So the rebuilt engine you buy might just have a crankshaft installed with its bearing journals so close to the edge of the wear tolerance that in another few thousand miles of normal use, it will be worn beyond that tolerance, or according to the manufacturer's specifications, *worn out*. The same thing applies to every moving part in the engine.

A freshly-overhauled engine, therefore, can conceivably be just about worn out when you get it. In just a few thousand miles, an engine like this could well be in worse shape than the one you replaced!

A factory assembly line is much better able to produce consistently high-quality engines than is any repair shop which has to make the many compromises necessary to enable it to handle hundreds of different makes and models of engines.

In all fairness, I have to say that somewhere out there, there might be a rebuilder who does a decent job. It's just that I have never been able to find him; and I've looked, too. I've had rebuilt engines from sources ranging from cheapo mass-production rebuild-factories to independent machine shops of high repute.

The information presented here is derived from experience with overhauled engines in cars that I have bought, taken in trade, or been associated with for other reasons; and from stories told by friends, relatives, business associates and customers. Based on all this input, it seems safe to say that it's a gamble to have any major repairs done to an aging engine.

Even one of the better rebuilt engines will rarely make it past fifty-thousand miles before it starts to blow smoke and develop funny noises. I have known very few overhauled engines which didn't make funny noises right out of the box. Lifter noises, timing-chain rattles, piston slap, wrist-pin rattles, you name it. Yet often, these engines fresh from the rebuilder that sounded pretty awful to me, didn't sound unusual to their owners at all. That must be why rebuilders get away with selling all those edgy engines: most customers either don't know the difference and a noisy engine sounds "normal" to them, or they just don't care. Or both.

Lots of owners of rebuilt engines have complained about excessive oil consumption and exhaust smoke right from the beginning. The garage usually gives the same stock answer: "We use such high-quality rings in our engines that they take longer to seat than ordinary rings. The engine will smoke and use oil for a while, and that's normal. Just ignore it for now, and when those rings seat, the engine will be better than new."

What is really being said is that you should just live with it until the warranty runs out, at which time it's your problem. An engine that smokes excessively when new will probably always smoke.

How About a New Engine?

So you forget about rebuilt engines and see about a brand new one from the dealer. OK, the car has a little over 100,000 miles on it. The engine is getting noisy, doesn't always start like it used to, and it is using oil. The blue haze coming from the exhaust can no longer be ignored. You go to the dealer.

After recovering from the shock that the new engine will cost over two thousand dollars installed (in many cases more than the car is worth), you ask just what will you get for the money. You are told that you get a factory-new block and heads: the entire engine, minus the carburetor or fuel injection, distributor, and accessories.

The accessories include all the emission-control hardware, alternator, air-conditioning compressor, belts, and in some cases, the water pump. You sign the order and the work begins. A few days later, you pick up your car, and after writing the big check, you drive it home. You notice that it still has that same funny hesitation upon acceleration that it did with the old engine!

And the next morning you notice that it still doesn't start like it ought to, and on the way to work, you stop at the dealer's. He tells you that those little glitches are in the carburetor, which as you know, has over 100,000 miles on it and really ought to be replaced. So, four hundred dollars later, you drive off again, only to have the 100,000 mile, $140 alternator go out.

And as soon as the hot days of summer are upon you, the 100,000 mile air-conditioning compressor goes out. Not to mention the old, tired emission-control hardware, which only causes occasional minor problems.

The Cost-Effective Solution

So, what's the solution? Remember way back when your car had only fifty-thousand miles on it? Remember how well it ran then, how dependable it was? Suppose that your car would have been involved in an accident then. Someone had run into the back of it and damaged it beyond repair. The body was damaged beyond repair, but the engine wasn't even touched.

Right now, today, in an auto salvage yard near you, there is a low-mileage engine that came out of a car identical to yours. The car was involved in an accident, but the engine came out unhurt.

That engine can be bought for about one-third the price of an overhaul; often less. And at that low price, it will include the carburetor or fuel-injection setup, alternator and all of the usual accessories. All those external parts and accessories will also be low-mileage. And since the engine is a complete assembly, your mechanic will be able to install it in a fraction of the time for a fraction of the cost that it would take to install a rebuilt or new block using all of your old, worn out external parts and accessories.

I would take my chances on just about any reasonably well-maintained factory 50,000 mile engine over any newly rebuilt engine. A factory new engine would outlast the used one, but consider the price of the new engine, and the eventual need to replace all of the expensive external parts.

Any time you are told that your aging auto needs a repair as major as a valve-job, or anything else requiring a fairly substantial disassembly of the engine, you are better off to replace the entire engine (complete with accessories) with a good, low-mileage used one.

Do not be intimidated by the words "wrecking yard." For the most part, there are no more wrecking yards. There are "auto-parts recyclers." The difference goes far beyond the name. Most of these businesses are expertly-managed, carefully-controlled operations with clean showroom/offices and computer-managed inventories. No more wading through ankle-deep grease to get to the filthy counter in a dingy little shack out in the middle of a sea of overturned, smashed cars.

At most inner-city dismantler's businesses, you won't even see any wrecked cars; just a nice, clean showroom and office, a well-run parts store. To purchase an engine from a recycler, you need only go to the one nearest you. If he doesn't have the exact one you need, he'll find it quickly on his "hotline." All of the parts recyclers are interconnected on one or more hot-lines and cooperate with one another in locating parts.

Your mechanic can handle the purchase of the used engine, so you never even need to get involved with that. However, if you aren't opposed to dealing with it, you will save the mechanic's price-markup on the engine, plus you'll get to ask the seller all the pertinent questions yourself, instead of getting the mechanic involved as middleman.

You could, of course, get on the phone and call around to the various businesses until you locate the right engine yourself. For any 1980 or newer engine, you should find a replacement of the same model year to insure that the emission control hardware will hook up directly. A different year engine might be basically identical and actually bolt up to your transmission, but if the emission control plumbing is even a little bit different, your mechanic might spend hours trying to make it work. Or worse yet, he might do his best and still not have it pass inspection.

Unless you feel qualified, this might be a time to ask for the help of a friend knowledgeable in things mechanical. Once you have located the correct engine, tell the salesperson that you want to look at the car it came out of. There is a good chance that the car in question is no longer in the yard; that it has already been completely scavenged for useful parts and the rest sent to the crusher.

But if possible, examine the car. Check the odometer, if it is still there. Look over the interior, and try to determine whether the car appears to have been taken care of. You'll have to ignore the damage caused by the wreck, of course, but usually it is apparent even in a wreck if a car has been abused. An abused body and interior is a pretty good indicator of the care received by the engine.

Look on the upper left corner of the windshield or the back edge of the driver's door for lube stickers which can give clues as to whether or not the engine was serviced properly (assuming that the car has a windshield and/or a driver's door). If you are lucky, you might even locate an engine which hasn't yet been removed from the car. Then you will have the opportunity to inspect the engine for oil leaks and general outside condition. (When engines are removed from the car, they generally get steam cleaned, effectively removing any evidence of leaks.)

The engine should look about like yours did with the same number of miles on it. The whole engine compartment should have about the same level of griminess, with no buildups of grease or visible evidence of oil leaks. There must be no rust stains, showing that the radiator had at one time boiled over. NEVER consider an engine if there is ANY evidence that it has EVER been overheated.

Check the inside of the radiator, or if it has already been removed, the inside of a radiator hose or hose fitting on the engine. It should be sparkling clean. There must be no evidence of oil, rust, or sooty black deposit.

Check the oil, breather cap, air-filter element just as if you were checking out a used car for possible purchase. Look in the glove box for repair receipts. Sometimes you can find entire repair histories in glove boxes of wrecks in auto-salvage yards.

What about exchangeability, the possibility of using an engine other than the exact make and model being replaced? As mentioned earlier, changing non-exact engines in cars newer than about 1980 is generally risky because of the emission-control hardware. There are federal laws prohibiting the alteration of this hardware, which makes the situation stickier yet.

Engines lacking the exact same emissions-control hardware *can* be exchanged using your old hardware, but this often means using your old carburetor or fuel injection and even the intake manifold. A consultation with the person who will do the work is in order here. Given the right price for the engine, it might be worthwhile.

But don't give up too easily finding the correct replacement. There are so many cars in these yards, and most of them are late model units, that the selection is amazing.

If all this seems like way too much hassle, then just let your mechanic find the engine for you. Between him and his preferred auto-salvage dealer's hotline, they can locate the right engine easily.

Engine Swaps

There is also a real market for other-than-exact engine replacements. Any older car qualifies, and the big market is for special-interest cars, which can include those which are of special interest to you only, as well as cars of great value. (See Chapter 5, Special Interest Cars.)

For example, say you have found an exceptionally nice 1966 Chev Impala. You like the car a lot, and everything about it is great except that it has 243,000 miles on the odometer and the engine is tired. Any small-block Chevrolet engine from a great range of years will bolt directly into this chassis.

Again, this might get way beyond what you even want to think about, but it's all easy stuff for a good, qualified mechanic, so let him deal with it. The possibilities of shuffling around engines, manifolds, carburetors and even transmissions on these older cars are endless. Many GM cars used the same engines for years, and are directly interchangeable.

If you find an older car in great shape but you aren't crazy about the zillion-horsepower, gas-guzzling engine, be comforted to know that most of these engines can be exchanged for the smaller, more efficient engines available for the car when it was new. Your local auto-dismantler/recycler has "interchange manuals" which tell exactly which engines will exchange directly with which others. Often employees at auto recyclers can tell you which engines will exchange by making a few simple adjustments or by installing both engine and transmission as a unit. Many older cars will accept a newer engine in every hookup except to the transmission. Assuming the car is worth spending the money, installing an engine/transmission assembly might solve the problem and give you a fresh transmission in the bargain.

Engines and transmissions are not the only parts which are often better purchased used. Ever wait too long for to do a brake reline and have to buy new rotors or drums? Ouch! Used, they are available for about one-third the price of new ones. It is good practice to consider your auto dismantler first whenever you need parts. Glass is a good example. If you have ever had the misfortune to have broken any uninsured auto glass and had to pay for it yourself, you know all about it. A door window for an bottom-of-the-line import can cost several hundred dollars. Without getting into the insanities of these kinds of prices, let's just say that a replacement can be purchased at a dismantler for about one-third of the new price. Often even less.

Even if you never do your own repairs, you can ask your repairperson to inquire about used parts first before buying any new ones. Used parts are usually just a phone call away from your mechanic's place of business. Most salvage yards will deliver parts to local repair businesses.

Minor Repairs

Most auto repairs, fortunately, aren't as serious as an engine overhaul. More often than not, when a car "breaks down," the problem is minor.

Most auto-repair facilities today are parts-replacing establishments. You bring in your car with a complaint of a specific problem, and the mechanic more or less blindly goes about replacing parts until, by accident, he eventually finds the one which was defective. Of course, you are charged for all of the parts, even though all but one were fine and didn't need replacement. And you are charged anywhere from $40 to $70 per hour for the "mechanic's" time.

An exception to the "blind replacement" syndrome is in the newer cars with electronic diagnostic equipment built-in. There are still no diagnosticians involved here, because the technician merely needs to plug the car into his diagnostic readout equipment, and it will tell him which component to replace. After the replacement, another readout is taken, and perhaps now another component will show up to be defective. Often, the diagnostic equipment gets confused and gives misleading reports to the technician, so unnecessary parts-replacement still goes on. (Really!) Even the shop manuals explain how the diagnostic equipment is limited in what it can diagnose, and that it will often display incorrect data. The bottom line is still: there is no substitute for a good *human* diagnostician!

Most of the electronic "black boxes" tucked away in all sorts of obscure places in our newer cars are a mystery to even the best repair specialists. If the shop's computer detects a malfunction in one of the black boxes, the black box gets replaced. They are sealed units, designed to be discarded for any malfunction. There is no repair possible, and most are protected either physically or electronically against any enterprising manufacturer duplicating them and selling them as aftermarket replacements for a reasonable price. Some of these little wonders cost several hundred dollars, and have about as much hardware tucked inside as in a ten-dollar radio.

Merchandising Tricks and Other Consumer Affairs

Many of these black boxes are also unnecessarily hidden in inaccessible corners of the car, like inside a quarter-panel where it will require several hours of shop time to remove most of the car's interior just to get at the thing.

And it's all part of modern merchandising. There is no legitimate reason for the astronomical prices of replacement auto parts. There is no reason why a grille, made of cheap PVC plastic and about as complex as a seventy-nine-cent ice-cube tray, should cost the consumer $180. There is no reason why a fender for a small import, a fender with as much metal in it as a $7.95 trash can, should cost the consumer $150.

And if that isn't bad enough, consider this: used to be, you could go buy a taillight lens for an average car for fifteen dollars or so. And that wasn't more than just a few years ago. Enter modern merchandising practices. The highly-paid executives who decide these practices determined that it was a shame that the consumer could get by with having to pay only fifteen dollars for this lens (which was about as complicated as many $1.39 kids' toys). To solve this dilemma, they simply glued the lens onto the very expensive taillight housing, which included the lamp sockets, wiring harness, and reflectors, and sold the whole thing as a unit. Now if you happen to crack your very (and unnecessarily) fragile taillight lens and go to the dealer for a replacement, you are told that this part is serviced only as a taillight unit, and you'll have to pay $165! And then you get to throw the perfectly good original lamp housing, with all its perfectly good hardware, in the trash. Be assured that this practice is not limited to taillight assemblies. It is becoming pervasive throughout this industry and others. At a time when it is of the utmost importance to conserve resources, these industry leaders bow to their god, The Bottom Line, by creating an ever-increasing throwaway society. Not only is this a grossly dishonorable business practice, it is environmentally obscene.

How do they get away with it? Simple. First of all, we have proven again and again to the merchandising executives that we will buy anything they tell us we need. Second, in almost all cases, who cares how much it costs to fix a car damaged in an accident? The insurance pays the bill, right?

Right. The consumer doesn't care. After all, with those high premiums that we have to pay, it serves the insurance company right to get nailed with a fat repair bill now and then, right?

Well, guess why the insurance premiums are so high? One has to wonder if it isn't a big conspiracy. The consumers don't care what the repairs cost because the insurance company pays the repair bills. The insurance companies don't care how high the repair bills get because they just raise our premiums to whatever level it takes to maintain their enormous profits. The body shops love it, because their profit is directly proportional to the repair bill.

So much for philosophy. Now, what can we do about it? *We can minimize the impact of this thievery in our own lives by become intelligent consumers.* By not letting someone sell us something we don't need. By buying used parts whenever possible. By properly maintaining our cars so that they won't need the parts in the first place.

Becoming intelligent consumers is what this book is all about. Some of the scams pulled on car-owners by larcenous repair facilities are hard to believe. And almost all of them would be impossible to pull off if the car-owner had even the most cursory knowledge of what made a car run.

If you just don't want to be bothered to learn about your vehicle and how it works, you still have the means to avoid the rip-off artist: get a second opinion. Or maybe a third, too.

You would be surprised at the different diagnoses you will get to the same problem presented to several different mechanics.

A Couple of Stories

My daughter took her car to a state-certified pollution-control inspection station for a mandatory inspection. The inspection cost her $36, and what she got for her money was a printout informing her that $90 worth of work was required to get the car to pass. After the $90 worth of work was completed, she would have to pay another $36 inspection fee, and then another $6 for the certificate she would need to present to the motor vehicles department. She called home for advice.

We told her write off the $36 to experience, ignore the advice she got for her money, and to try another inspection station . . . but first to *ask around for referrals*. It worked. The next place did the same inspection to the same car, using the same state-mandated performance specifications, and with the simple adjustment of the idle-speed screw on the carburetor, the car passed with flying colors. No repairs needed.

She could have saved herself $36, an anxious phone call and a lot of time by asking for referrals first. Had she elected to go with the advice of the first shop, she would have dropped $178 for a service which was overpriced at $36. Clearly, this is thievery. The solution? *Ask for referrals!*

An auto dealer friend recently told me about a late-model Chevy pickup that he bought at an auction. It ran fine under most conditions but wouldn't idle smoothly. He sent it to the local Chevrolet dealer for the necessary repair. The repair bill from that dealer was nearly $600, and he allegedly replaced almost every component in the engine's pollution-control systems. The engine ran a little more smoothly, but it still was not right. After a week, it ran as roughly as it did when the dealer bought it.

He then took it to a large independent garage with all sorts of fancy diagnostic equipment. There he was told that the engine "probably" needed a valve job. After the dealer's own mechanic did a compression check which indicated no need of a valve job, the truck was sent to yet one more garage, a small local shop where the owner had a reputation as a skillful diagnostician. He found and replaced a defective vacuum hose, which fixed the problem. The charge? Twenty-four dollars labor and a dollar for the hose. This mechanic was one whose name comes up often when asking around for referrals.

Here's a good one. You leave your two-year-old, eighteen-thousand-mile Oldsmobile at the body shop for a fender-bender repair. The shop owner has one just like it, only his has ninety-five thousand miles on it. It still runs OK, but it is getting tired. After the shop closes for the night, he pulls your car into the back room, removes the engine, and replaces it with the engine from his car. The body-repair job gets done, and you pick up your car, and not until many months later do you start getting messages from your engine that it seems to be wearing out prematurely. What really happened will never occur to you.

Sounds preposterous? You bet, but it happens. And not with only engines, either.

In many cases, garages have specialty areas in which they abuse their customer's confidences. For example, some mechanics will sell you a battery no matter what is wrong with your car. Even if you leave it for an oil change, they'll at least *try* to sell you that battery.

Some will just try a verbal approach, implying that your present battery is very tired and might leave you stranded at any time, and that you really ought to take advantage of this opportunity to buy a battery at the "sale" price instead of waiting until you're stuck on the freeway in the middle of the night in a rainstorm, etc.

Others use a more aggressive approach. You leave your car for an oil change or some other service. A couple of hours later, you return, and while paying the bill, the manager informs you that he had to jump-start your car to pull it into the shop. He says that you must have a bad battery. You tell him that the battery is only a year old and you've never had any problem with it. Well, he says, then it's probably shorted out. That can happen at any time with no warning. Let's go check it out, he says. You follow him to the car, and he uses his battery tester to show you how the battery is indeed nearly dead. Shorted cell, he says, and boy are you ever in luck. He's running a battery sale right now and he can let you have a brand new battery for only $49.95, installed. He could, of course, just charge up your old battery and you could maybe get by for a few more days . . .

When you left your car, the nice mechanic just put a big load on your battery to make sure that if you tried to start the car, it wouldn't. He's really good at this trick, having perfected it for during the last ten years.

Rather than devote this entire chapter to case histories of auto-repair thievery, I suggest that you just consider your own past experiences with auto-repair facilities, and talk them over with any friend who owns a car. You're certain to hear as many horror stories as you have the time and patience for. Very unfortunately, this industry deserves all the bad press it gets, and then some.

In most states, the garages even have legal protection to conduct their thievery. A mechanic or garage can hold your car under a legal mechanic's lien until his bill is paid. If the bill gets disputed in court, *he* is the expert witness in his own behalf. After all, what do you know about it... you're just a consumer. And more than likely, so will be the judge.

A word of advice: if you find that you have been unquestionably ripped off, do not stop payment on the check with which you paid the garage! File a claim in small-claims court to recover your money, but don't stop payment. Most states treat a stop-payment as fraud, assuming your intent to have been to make the garagekeeper believe you were paying for a service which you had no intention of doing. A stop-payment can backfire to the point where the garagekeeper ends up suing you, or at the very least, having your complaint dismissed.

Your best defense is to know your car at least well enough to be able to detect a repair diagnosis which is obviously wrong. Failing that, I recommend that you get at least two different opinions before signing the repair order.

This might make you want to run right down to your nearest diagnostic clinic. You know, those fancy, computer-equipped facilities which support their claims of honesty by telling you that since they sell only their diagnostic expertise and no parts or repairs, it is not in their interest to tell you of nonexistent problems.

It has been my experience that diagnostic clinics are quite capable of giving a "worn out" report on a brand new car. They can also overlook serious discrepancies, as well as give diagnoses inconsistent with other diagnostic centers and with reality. There is no substitute for a skilled, if hard-to-find diagnostician.

Disclaimer: Again, this is a generalization based upon lots of experience; my own and that of many customers, business associates and friends. For all I know, there just might be a diagnostic clinic out there somewhere from which you could get some useful information.

Another Daughter-Story

One day, my daughter (same one) called to say she was going to drive the 500 miles to come for a visit. Because her car seemed to be using a little more gas than normal, she said that she would take it into a nearby shop for a checkup before leaving. It was a large diagnostic center, she said, and it looked impressive: lots of new, expensive cars and flashy test-equipment.

She took her car in, and the results of her checkup told her that her car needed a new oxygen-sensor in the catalytic converter. They told her, "It will cost about $125, and if you're dumb enough to drive the car home the way it is, we can't guarantee that it won't catch on fire!" My daughter called me first. I asked her if the "ECS" light on her dashboard was on. It wasn't. Aside from excessive gas consumption, the car was running just fine.

Since it was highly unlikely that her fairly-new, 30,000-mile car really needed an oxygen sensor, I advised her to drive the car up for her visit, that I would check it out when she got here. Even if it needed an oxygen sensor, the car would run just fine if possibly using a bit more gas than it should.

The problem? The automatic choke was not opening fully. The oxygen sensor checked out within factory tolerances. And an inexpensive voltmeter was all that was required to determine it, too.

Had my daughter listened to the high-pressure sales tactics of her garage-mechanic, she would have been sold a $125 job which was unnecessary and *her car still would not have been repaired.* Unfortunately, this sort of incompetence and/or dishonesty is pervasive.

Protect Yourself

When you do finally decide on the shop that is going to repair your car, never leave the car until you have received a copy of the repair order. Read the fine print. Make sure that the repair order doesn't have any loopholes which authorize the shop to do any work beyond what you authorized *under any circumstances*. If the full price of the repair cannot be stated on the repair order, make certain that the order states that you will be notified of the price before the work is done. You may elect to put a dollar-ceiling on the work above which you must be notified before doing the job. Make it known that you want to inspect both the removed parts and the packages from any replacement parts. (Some shops keep an inventory of damaged or worn parts just to have them on hand to show to people who insist on inspecting replaced parts. The parts you are shown may be from such an inventory.)

It is very unfortunate to have to go to these lengths to avoid getting taken by the many unscrupulous facets of our automobile industry. And it's even more unfortunate that women seem to be the prime targets for much of the overcharging.

All of this also places an unwarranted burden on the *honest* individuals trying to operate within the system. For them, it is truly demeaning to have everyone who comes through the door view them as thieves and cheats. Happily, the honest businessmen seem to have no trouble in attracting more word-of-mouth referrals than they can handle. It is our sincere recommendation that if you are lucky enough to be told by several sources of such a repairperson, that you follow through and give this person your auto-service business. And tell your friends!

How to Find Your Mechanic

So where do you look for a competent mechanic? *Ask for referrals!* Ask as many people as you can, and when the same name starts coming up again and again, that's your mechanic. It's a simple process, and it really does work. The word gets around, and people who get treated fairly like to share their experience with others. Just asking around, "Do you know of a good, dependable and honest mechanic?" will eventually produce that repeated name.

A *super-mechanic* diagnoses problems using his expertise and common sense, as opposed to the *average* mechanic, who likely just starts replacing parts (at your expense) until he accidentally fixes the problem.

There is no substitute for expertise: a good mechanic, one who is also a good diagnostician, is a problem-solver far superior to a bunch of robots in possession of a whole shop full of impressive diagnostic equipment.

Factory-Trained Mechanics

Many people believe that if they take their Chevy to the Chevy dealer, or their Honda to the Honda dealer, they're safe, with "factory-trained" mechanics.

Most new-car dealers hire their mechanics out of the same union hall as does everyone else. The guy who services your Toyota in the Toyota dealer's shop might have been doing Fords last week. For the most part, the notion of factory-trained mechanics is a myth. And on top of that, dealership garages generally have the most expensive shop rates and parts prices.

In all fairness, there are some dealerships that take pride in their repair facilities and make certain that their staff is competent. There are even some which won't intentionally sell you unnecessary parts and service. They are rare, however, so unless you get abundant recommendations and referrals to a specific dealership, independent shops are the way to go. And abundant recommendations are the way to go in either case.

Certified Mechanics

There are consumer organizations that will advise you to trust only "certified mechanics." My experience has made it clear that a certificate is no substitute for experience and natural aptitude. I know several mechanics who are superb diagnosticians. The have no certificates. Instead, they love cars, they love problem-solving, and they've made a career out of learning everything there is to learn about their trade.

I know other mechanics who are certified but who've had little practical experience. Some of them got their certifications just because it made finding a job easier. I'm sure you know of some college grads who received their "certificates" and still can't support themselves, right? Well, it's just like that in the automotive world.

There are good and not-so-good mechanics, and some of each have certificates; some don't. One fairly good indication is if a mechanic has a whole wall full of certificates. At least then its safe to assume that he's serious about his craft. It still doesn't mean that he's good, though.

If certification means something special to you, then by all means, find a certified mechanic. But be sure to find one certified in the exact field that you need. For example, there are mechanic's schools that specialize in engines, transmissions, electronic fuel-injection systems, brake systems, and so on. A mechanic with a general certificate doesn't necessarily know anything at all about computer-controlled, electronic fuel-injection systems. Or automatic transmissions.

HOW TO KEEP IT RUNNING (NEARLY) FOREVER

To expect our cars to run (nearly) forever, we must give them back something in return. Without a doubt, regular scheduled maintenance is what it takes.

Many years ago, when having your car last a long time was still fashionable, car makers would use high-mileage examples of their cars to demonstrate the value of their product. They would run an ad showing this guy with his twenty-year-old car, with

350,000 miles on the odometer. The owner would say how this car still had the original engine and had never needed any major repairs. Nowadays, this kind of advertising would be worthless, not to mention counterproductive to the billions of dollars spent trying to talk us into buying a new throw-away car every year.

The point? The 350,000 mile car wasn't necessarily a better car than some other make; most cars respond remarkably well to good maintenance.

Sure there are exceptions. There are the lemons that you've already smoked out by asking your favorite mechanic about them. But since *you* know better now, and you're only going to buy a car that has earned a reputation for exceptional reliability, yours will be one that will respond well to your TLC.

Periodic Maintenance

Keeping engine oil clean is the most important of all maintenance items. Engine oil should be changed every 3000 miles. The oil filter should be changed at the same time. If you have a garage do your oil changes, make sure that they do the normally associated service at the same time. This includes checking all fluid levels (brake fluid, transmission oil, coolant, battery water (if it's the kind of battery where this is possible), and windshield washer fluid.

At every third oil change and service (or whenever specified in your owner's guide or shop manual), chassis-lube points should be serviced. Most late-model cars have very few lube fittings to service; most of the parts that require lubrication are permanently lubricated and sealed at the factory. Your mechanic will know where to find the lube fittings, and if you do your own servicing, they're clearly identified in the manual.

When you buy a used car, check the condition of all of the hoses and belts in the engine compartment. Belts (water-pump, alternator, air-conditioning and other accessory drive-belts), and heater and radiator hoses, last about three or four years in the extremely hot environment of an engine compartment. After that, they're candidates for failure even if they still look OK. It is best to have them all replaced, *unless it is obvious* that they are already recent replacements. I've seen a lot of hoses that looked just fine develop little leaks at the most inopportune moments. Belts are usually more obvious, in that they will show their condition. A tired belt will show cracks, especially on the underside that rides in the pulleys. The nominal expense of simply replacing all of them is worth the peace of mind you get from knowing that this problem isn't going to happen to you. Thereafter, remember that they're good for about another three or four years. Tip: if you have a mechanic change the hoses, be firm about having them all replaced. I've known shops to just "forget" the little, obscure heater and bypass hoses that are difficult to reach.

A shop manual is an excellent investment and a valuable resource, whether or not you do your own service. The manuals available at most auto-supply stores, while not as complete as the factory manuals, will do nicely for most car owners. (See Chapter 17.)

Once in a while, like every six months or so, open your hood, doors and trunk and apply a little oil to the hinges and latch mechanisms of each. (Some regular engine oil in a hardware-store oil can works well for this.) These are often neglected areas in even professional garage service procedures, and they're important to the long life of your car. They're especially important if you live in a coastal area where everything has a tendency to rust.

Rust and Corrosion

Other considerations for coastal area cars (or if you live where roads are salted in winter) are keeping the car away from the corrosives as much as possible, and washing it after exposure. Keeping the car away from exposure isn't always possible, but the damage can be minimized by some simple measures. For example, if you're going to the beach, don't park where the direct salt-laden wind will find your car. Park a block away, or at least behind a building. It really does make a difference! After the day at the beach, wash your car with plenty of soapy water. Squirt a liberal amount of dish soap on your carwash brush or sponge, and then apply it all over the car along with lots of water, paying special attention to places where water can run down into cracks, like the edges of the hood and trunk, and around the doors. Let lots of soapy water run down in those places and then follow it with a good rinse.

If you live where your car is always exposed to salty air, or even the acid air of industrial areas, do the above wash frequently. I use this technique on my cars here in Hawaii, and I have very few problems with rust.

Of course, the best approach is to keep your car garaged, or even under a car port. But even that won't stop rust and corrosion if the car isn't washed frequently.

Sun damage is most often seen as cracked dash tops and rotted upholstery on the back seat and package shelf. Top edges of door panels fade and crack from continued sun exposure, too, and all of this can be minimized by keeping the car under cover as much as possible. If this sort of thing is important to you, go to the extra effort of finding a shady place to park, even if it means walking an extra block. It all makes a difference!

Tire Maintenance

Tire life can be doubled by regular maintenance: rotation and correct air-pressure. Make sure that radial tires are switched back and forth *only* on the same side of the car. They should never be switched to the opposite side, because the tires can be damaged by alternately running them in the opposite direction. Correct air pressure is that pressure at which your tires wear evenly. Manufacturer's recommendations are a good starting point. (The pressures listed on the tires themselves are *maximums*; they are *not* the recommended pressures. Recommended pressures are normally shown on a sticker in either door jamb.) From there, watch the way they wear, especially the front tires. If they're wearing faster in the middle of the tread, they are *over*inflated. *Drop* the pressure two or three pounds. If they're wearing faster on the outside edges of the treads, they are *under*inflated. *Add* two or three pounds pressure. After any pressure changes, check the tire wear again after about a thousand miles. It's that simple.

Interior

The interior of your car can be kept like new with a few simple techniques. The first, in my opinion, is to use your car for transportation, not as a restaurant! Food spills have ruined more upholstery and carpets than anything else. If you do eat or drink in your car (and we all do once in a while), if at all possible, clean up any spills before they get a chance to dry. Use gentle soap, like dish soap or an upholstery shampoo. Applying some Scotch-gard® (or equivalent) after the cleaned spot is dry, will prevent that spot from attracting more than its fair share of normal grime. Frequent vacuuming of the carpets and seats is an important step in keeping them looking young. Vacuuming the seats gets dirt out of the nooks and crannies, where it tends to become impacted and difficult to remove after a while.

When you clean any of the hard plastic parts of the interior, especially the dashboard, instrument panel, radio and heater controls, use only a gentle soap on a slightly dampened cloth. Never use a strong cleaner like 409® or even window cleaners (most of which contain ammonia). These cleaners can quickly take the simulated chrome and lettering off of the plastic!

If you often transport a carload of kids, it becomes a little more difficult to keep your car's interior spotless. A little more difficult, but certainly not impossible. Seat-belt laws help us a lot here, because at least strapped-in kids are going to stay seated. Setting some firm rules about not eating in the car (no exceptions; you can't either when anybody's watching) is the best way to prevent the otherwise inevitable ("Oops, I'm sorry!") accidents.

Driving Habits: Brakes

Driving habits also determine the life of your car, particularly of the mechanical parts. Remember to keep your foot off of the brake pedal unless you are intentionally applying the brakes! When you're going down a long, steep hill, shift into whatever gear will allow the car to coast at your desired speed without using the brakes at all. If you do need the brakes on a long hill, apply short, intermittent pressure on the pedal instead of light pressure for long periods. Continued pressure on the brakes, even if it's a light pressure, heats up the brake linings and/or pads to the point where they not only wear rapidly, but get so hot that they will warp the brake rotors. (Another expensive and entirely avoidable fix.) Hot brakes also are relatively ineffective in stopping your car. If you "ride" your brakes all the way down a steep hill, you just might not be able to stop at all when you get to the bottom.

Have your front brake pads inspected whenever the tires are rotated. The pads are exposed for inspection when the front wheels are removed. Rear brakes should be inspected when the front brakes need service. Rear linings generally outlast fronts two or three to one.

All disc brakes have an "audible wear indicator" built in. It's nothing more than a little metal clip that starts to drag on the brake rotor when the pads are worn to the critical point. If you hear a little squeaky-scrapey noise whenever you apply the brakes, you need new pads. Don't wait until next week, or even until your next paycheck! Replacing pads in a timely manner is an inexpensive job. Waiting until the pads are worn a bit more can turn it into a frighteningly expensive repair.

Transmissions

Neither standard nor automatic transmissions like to be unnecessarily down-shifted. Some people shift down through each gear every time they come to a stop. Don't! This practice accomplishes nothing besides putting a lot of extra wear and tear on the transmission. Shift down into the next lower gear when you need the engine braking, or compression, for going down hills. When you driving on straight and level roads, just let the car coast to a stop by taking your foot off the gas far enough ahead of the next signal that a gentle brake application will bring you to a stop.

Got a standard shift? Be gentle. Again, minimize downshifting to when it's necessary. The fastest wearing parts in most transmissions are the synchronizers. Their job is to bring all the rotating parts to the same speed so that the gears will mesh easily and quietly. When you shift gears gently, the wear is negligible. When you shift gears really quickly, the synchronizers are forced to exert their maximum capability, and in so doing, they wear excessively. The more you do it, the more rapidly they wear, and the sooner your transmission will need expensive repairs.

Hot-Rod Driving

Another wear-and-tear no-no is full-throttle acceleration. If you need it to get out of a tight spot or onto an on-ramp, go for it. But remember that the wear on every part of your car from the engine to the drive wheels (and tires) is greatly increased by full-throttle acceleration. Full-throttle upshifts with an automatic transmission will cause premature failure of the transmission. You're also wasting a lot of gas and wearing out tires prematurely, too.

Flying around corners is another expensive habit. Taking corners at higher-than-comfortable speeds can easily cut the life of your front tires in half. If you have to do a lot of driving on twisty roads, try to take it easy. Tires are expensive, and the corners is where they get the most wear. Driving on a lot of twisty roads is also a good reason to pay special attention to rotating those tires. As soon as the fronts and rears show different wear patterns, it's time to switch them.

The Clutch

Keep that clutch foot on the floor unless you're actively using the clutch! Some people just kind of leave their left foot lightly resting on the clutch pedal. Don't! Any time your foot is touching the clutch pedal, the clutch-release bearing is forced to spin. This bearing is designed for the proper *intermittent* use of the clutch, and if you keep it spinning for long periods of time, it wears out quickly. Expensive fix. Make sure that your clutch is properly adjusted. It's a real simple test that you can do in five seconds yourself. (See Chapter 15.)

Never, ever use the clutch to keep your car on a hill, like when you're waiting for a light to change. Use the *brake* to hold the car on the hill, and the clutch to get the car moving again. Any time you are "slipping the clutch," as in using it to keep the car from rolling back down a hill, you are doing incredible damage to the clutch, and shortening its life by a great amount. A few seconds of slipping the clutch like that can create more wear than thousands of miles of normal driving. In addition, the tremendous heat generated by a slipping clutch can warp the surfaces of the flywheel and pressure-plate, again meaning expensive repairs. I've seen lots of clutches last well over 100,000 miles, and others than didn't make it to 30,000. It's up to you!

Know your Car

Get to know your car. Be a conscious driver. Pay attention to what your well-behaved, normally running car sounds and feels like, so that when something isn't right, you'll notice it right away. And when you do notice that something is out of the ordinary, fix it before it becomes a major hassle. Most of the time, paying attention to your car's cry for help, such as a little squeak or rumble or whine that you've never noticed before, will allow you to fix a potential problem before it becomes a real one.

Get in the habit of doing an occasional visual scan of your dashboard. If your car has gauges for oil pressure, charging and temperature, make a note of the readings on these gauges when everything is normal. After a few times of looking at them, you'll become familiar enough with what "normal" looks like, that your eye will immediately catch a gauge-reading that is *not* normal. When a gauge reads out of its normal range of operation, it's time to figure out why. Don't wait until something breaks; the abnormal reading is giving you fair warning that something is about to! If your car has only warning lights and no gauges, remember that a warning light is telling you that there is something seriously wrong *right now*. Pull over and stop as soon as you can safely do so.

I've had people bring me cars that were making some terrible noise along with not running worth a hoot. I'd ask them how long has it been making that noise, and the usual comment would be, "what noise?" These are usually the same folks who complain about their cars being undependable . . .

In summary, do your scheduled maintenance, teach yourself to be a conscious driver, and immediately heed your car's pleas for attention. If you do, you can expect your car to perform at its maximum potential. Never let yourself fall into the trap of "waiting until later" to respond to your car's needs. *Later* almost always equates with *more expensive*.

If you follow the advice in this book, it's unlikely that you'll ever have to deal with an emergency roadside repair. In my nearly one-million miles of driving literally hundred of different cars, I've had one episode of having a car break in the middle of nowhere. An alternator belt broke. (I had a spare, and tools.)

Use the Check List (Appendix) when you go car shopping, make a great deal on your favorite car, and give it some TLC. Drive consciously, heed the call when your car asks for help, do your scheduled maintenance, and it will look and run like the day you bought it for as long as you care to keep it.

Happy motoring!

About the Author

Skip Thomsen, born and raised (as Hans Paul Thomsen) in the San Francisco Bay Area, has been a car nut since he was sixteen, and that was a long time ago. Since then, he's owned hundreds of different vehicles and several repair and body shops in both California and Oregon. He was a licensed auto dealer in both states for many years. His shops earned the reputation of doing some of the finest work available. Many of his customers were owners of classic, racing and special-interest autos. His mechanical expertise has served him well in building successful show- and race-cars from the ground up. He believes that contrary to popular myth, mechanical breakdowns are not a fact of life.

Over the years in various auto businesses, Thomsen observed that women are regularly seen as easy victims for every kind of moneymaking scam imaginable. In recent years, "feeling helpless" came up often when listening to women talk about their auto-related dealings.

After his retirement from the auto business in 1989, he started formulating a car book for women who want an excellent car at a reasonable price and who feel uneasy about dealing with dealers, mechanics and others in the trade.

In 1988, Thomsen wrote a car-savvy book similar to The Intelligent Woman's (Used) Car Book, but directed to a general audience. It was published by National Information Bureau (Acadia Marketing) in Los Angeles, a mail-order book sales company, as Car Buyer's Handbook. It sold 23,000 copies in the six months before the company went out of business. He has done nothing with that title since then, choosing instead to focus on The Intelligent Woman's (Used) Car Book.

Thomsen has successfully self-published two how-to books in other fields and is marketing them through his company, Oregon Wordworks, in Eugene, Oregon. He has also written numerous magazine articles on various how-to topics, including several on dealing with cars. Reviews of his writing consistently commend him for his ability to make complex topics clear and easy to understand.

During 1988-89, he and his wife published an arts-and-entertainment guide called Elixir! for the

North Oregon Coast area. A paper of 16-20 pages with a circulation of five-thousand copies, it included a variety of articles, fiction, and poetry concerning Oregon Coast issues. It was well received and got good reviews. It was put to sleep when the couple moved to Hawaii in 1993.

Thomsen is considering a future book on buying, owning and enjoying special-interest autos. Covered to some extent in Chapter 5, this exciting field of motoring allows one to drive a luxury dream-car or perhaps an as-new, vintage collectible for less than the price of a new economy car. It also eliminates the huge expense of depreciation, and in the bargain can bring fun back into driving.

Mr. Thomsen is now happily living in rural Hawaii with his two cats and his twelve-year-old convertible that has over 100,000 miles on it and still drives like a new car.

Quick Reference Guide

The information in the Quick Reference Guide is identical to the Pocket Check List supplied with this book. It is intended as a guide in assessing a possible purchase, and presumes that you have read (at least most of) the book! The items on this list are very brief and are just reminders of things to look over. Page numbers are included for ease of referring back to the book, if necessary. The referenced text gives the full description of how to deal with each step. The page numbers shown are the *starting points* of the info you're looking for so don't stop at that page! Remember, it takes only a short while to do a thorough inspection, and you'll enjoy your <u>good</u> car for years!

Body & Paint

General Appearance: is it well kept or is there lots of minor damage?

Complete repaint clues: check masking on moldings, under edges of windshield gasket or trim, in door jambs, under edges of hood, trunk & cowl screens. (217)

Spot-painting clues: look down sides for irregularities, dull spots, sand-scratch. Catch reflections; surfaces should be uniform and shiny. (220)

Panel fits (very important): check for uniform gaps between panels, general panel alignment. Misalignments, especially several on the same side indicate structural damage. Check carefully! (222)

Doors: check for fit, alignment and sag. (228)

Interior: seats & upholstery condition, broken-down driver's seat (sit on it!), power-seat mechanisms, recliners. Check brake and clutch pedals for wear. Check carpets. Look under floor mats (back seat area, too), door panels, arm rests, dashboard for wear and breakage. Try every switch and gadget. (229)

Glass: carefully check windshield for sand-pitting and small chips or cracks. Impossible to inspect dirty or wet windshield. Check all windows full up and down.

Mechanical

Under the hood: check radiator coolant for condition and quantity. (238) Check engine, transmission, and power-steering-pump oil for quantity and condition. (242) Ignore the salesman and anything he tells you! (236) Determine whether or not you are starting with a cold engine.

Before starting the engine: get in the car, turn on the ignition to check warning lights and gauges. All warning lights should come on before starting engine. If any do not, find out why. Oil pressure and volt meter should read zero, ammeter should be centered. There may be a volt meter or an ammeter, but not both. (245)

Start engine. Warning lights should go off immediately. Oil pressure should come up to a high reading, ammeter should go nearly to full charge and then taper off, volt meter should read 14-16 volts. (246)

Warning lights? Charge-light flicker at low idle with accessories on is OK, but must stop with slight increase on engine speed. Oil pressure light must stay off. (246)

With engine running: oil pressure should read steady at the high end of "normal" range, dropping to "normal" as engine warms up. Ammeter/voltmeter should indicate a slight charge with engine warmed up. (250)

Air Conditioning: try all settings. Full-on A/C must blow very cold.

Power steering test: at idle, briskly turn steering wheel fully from one side to the other, check for squealing belt, pulsations felt in steering wheel. (268)

Driving Test

Engine: watch gauges and/or idiot lights: warmed up oil pressure must still be normal, slight drop OK at idle. Oil light must never come on, even at idle. Engine temp. gauge must stay at normal, even during fast or hilly driving, or in traffic. (264)

Cold engine: smooth acceleration, no hesitation on acceleration. Check for smooth operation at both idle and driving. (264)

Highway tests: at highway speed, hold lightly or let go of steering wheel to check for wheel vibrations. Let go of wheel; car should pull slightly toward crown of road. (265)

No crown, car should track straight. (265)

Braking: (preferably) downhill, brake hard; check for pulling to one side or the other, check for pulsation/vibration felt in brake pedal. (267)

Automatic transmission: accelerate to about 35 mph. Check for smooth shifts. No jerking, clunking or noises at shift points. Check reverse, too! (244)

Manual transmission: before starting out, check clutch-pedal free-play. Driving tests: smooth engagement with pedal about half way up from floor...no more. Be sure to try the clutch on a hill or steep driveway. Try it backing up, too. (269)

Check for slipping clutch: holding the gas pedal steady at 25-30 mph, momentarily (like just barely push it in and let it out immediately) depress the clutch at a very light throttle. The clutch should re-engage smoothly and immediately with no slipping or engine racing. (270)

Synchros: accelerate from a stop, shifting through each gear with a quick, positive shift. Should shift smoothly with no gear-grinding. From top gear, while slowing back down, shift down through each gear. Again, smooth gear-engagement and no grinding. (272)

Be sure to include stop & go, steep hills, and some highway driving. Observe gauges and/or idiot lights regularly. Temp must remain constant. Front-wheel or four-wheel drive: check CV joints. (274)

After the Drive

Park and leave the engine running. Rev it up (easy!) and check for exhaust smoke. Look at exhaust pipe. Should be no moisture, no black smudgy film in the pipe. Exhaust should sound smooth; no misses. (252)

Under the hood: check for blowby with PCV valve pulled out and oil filler removed. Inspect bottom of filler cap. **Shut off engine.** Inspect inside of air cleaner. Should be no oil visible anywhere inside. Hoses and belts: with engine hot, no bulges in hoses. Check belts for tension and cracks. Edgy belts and hoses indicate no maintenance has been done. (252)

Underneath: Check all four tires for uneven wear and condition. (237) Look for signs of oil leaks. Check condition of exhaust system. On front-wheel drive cars, check condition of CV joint boots. (253) Hoist car if possible. (254)

Index

A
accessory drive-belts ... 325
adjuster, insurance .. 181
aftermarket parts ... 176
air cleaners 253
air-conditioning 33
Alfa Romeo 12, 103
ammeter 247
Anti-locking brakes .. 38
AS-IS 161
assessing needs 9, 11
auto loans 156
automatic transmission
... 26, 239, 244, 269, 332
AutoNation 72

B
band-aid repair 289
bank loan-officers ... 156
beat the game 67
belts 325
big cars 100
"black boxes" 305
body repairs 217

Blue-Book tricks 155
brake rotors, pads ... 257
brakes 267
Buy American 21
buying a lifestyle 49

C
CarMax 72
certified mechanics . 320
charge light 247
check It out 215
clubs 121
clutch 270, 334
consumer protection 160
cooling system 239
cooling-system 241
corrosion 327
cruise control 28
curbstoners 84
CV Joints 253, 274

D
dealer auctions 137
defensive driving 36
diagnostic clinics ... 315

349

diesel cars 209
driving habits: brakes
. . . . 331
E
economy car 93
emotional decisions . . 50
engine 238, 245
engine oil 239, 242
engine swapping
. . . . 123, 301
estimates 184
exotic cars 12, 120
expenses 99
extended warranty . . 166
F
factory radio 32
factory warranties . . . 165
factory-trained
  mechanics 319
financing 189, 192
find your mechanic . . 318
flat tire 285
freeway test 265
FTC Sticker 159
full-size car 20
G
gas mileage . . . 14, 16, 93

gauges 248
getting estimates 184
H
Hemmings Motor News
. . . . 113
hi-milers 39
high performance 13
hoses and belts . 252, 325
hot-rod driving 333
I
idiot lights 245
informed customer . . 146
insurance 13, 173
interior 15, 329
investment autos   116
J
Jaguars 12
K
Kelley Blue Book . . . 150
L
leak 254
Lease returns 143
M
maintenance 323
major repairs 286
manual transmissions
. . . . 272

mid-sized cars 19
miles per dollar 101
minivans 11
minor repairs 304
Mustangs . 103, 109, 119

N
'Net surfing 121
new car 197
new vs. used 197

O
oil filters 243
oil-pressure gauge ... 247
oil-pressure light 246
options 22
overhauled engines126, 291
owner's organizations 121
owner's manual 287

P
panel alignment 222
planned obsolescence
 201
power brakes 25
power mirrors 30
power steering 24
power windows 29

private party 83
protect yourself 317

R
radiator 239
rear defrost 32
rebuilt wrecks   139
repaints 217
repairs 111
reputable dealer 67
roadside emergencies
 284
rust 226, 327
rust repairs 227

S
safety issues 36
shocks 258
shop manuals .. 283, 326
special-interest car
                 103, 190
sports cars 11
spot painting 220
staying in control 68
steering 268
super-mechanic 319
survival skills 73
synchros 272

T

temperature gauge 247
test drive 263
Thunderbirds 107
tilt wheel 27
tires 237
tire maintenance 328
trade-ins 131
transmissions 332
Triumphs 12
tuneups 17
"Turn-Over" System 59

U

under the car 235
under the hood 235
Used Car Guide 150
Used-Car Superstores 72

W

wagons 11
warning lights 245
warranties 165
when it breaks 279
wholesale auction 138
wrecks 216

Z

zero down 190

If you would like to order additional copies of
The Intelligent Woman's (Used) Car Book
here are several ways to do it.
(Additional copies are $14.95)

On-Line Credit-Card orders:
ALTERNATIVE BOOKS SUPERSTORE
http://www.TheAlternativeBookshop.com

Toll-Free, Credit-Card Phone Orders:
UPPER ACCESS BOOKS
1-800-356-9315
Website:
http://www2.upperaccess.com/upperaccess/uapweb.htm
(or type "upper access books" into a search-engine.)

Direct-from-Publisher Mail-Order
OREGON WORDWORKS
P.O. Box 231091
Portland, OR 97281
(Please include $2 S&H)

For more info on **OREGON WORDWORKS**
visit http.//www.mailbooks.com